Libellus de Historia

Latin History Reader
for use with

Latin for Children: Primer B

Acknowledgements

Classical Academic Press would like to thank **William R. Nethercut** for his expertise and care in editing this text.

Libellus de Historia

Latin History Reader for use with
Latin for Children: Primer B

Classical Academic Press
3920 Market Street
Camp Hill, PA 17011
www.ClassicalAcademicPress.com

ISBN: 1-60051-010-8
EAN: 9781600510106

Book design & cover by:
Robert A. Baddorf

"Cui dono lepidum novum libellum . . ."
-Catullus

With immense gratitude for my husband,
Bryan Moore, whose passion for God's truth is my
inspiration. Without your love and support I never
could have completed this little book.

Latin For Children, Primer B
LATIN READER

Contents

1

Contents

Contents

* N.B.

As this reader was designed to supplement <u>Latin for Children, Primer B</u>, the following grammar is assumed for all stories:

- 1st & 2nd conjugation, present system
  (i.e., present, imperfect, future tenses)
- 1st & 2nd declension nouns and adjectives
- irregular verbs *esse* & *īre*
- use of the nominative case (subject, predicate) and accusative case (direct object)
- simple prepositional phrases using both the accusative and ablative cases

Latin is a language unlike any other. One uses it not merely to communicate with others regarding the happenings of the present, but also as a key to unlock the secret treasures of the past. It is therefore, with greatest delight that we share with you this little book of 32 Latin stories that tell a few tales of treasures past. From the conversion of St. Augustine to the explorations of Marco Polo, from the re-trial of Joan of Arc to the Spanish Inquisition, students will discover some of history's most exciting events while applying the grammar tools of Latin that they have acquired.

Each story is keyed to the Latin grammar and vocabulary taught in <u>Latin for Children, Primer B</u> and the history taught through the <u>Veritas Press Middle Ages, Renaissance, and Reformation Series</u>. While the reader was originally conceived as a supplemental text to enhance the learning experience of the student using these curricula, it is not necessary to use either of them to benefit from and enjoy this reader. This little book has a user-friendly format in order to provide full support for even the most novice Latin teachers, regardless of the curriculum they choose.

Several helpful features are included to make this text easy to use by students, teachers, and parents. First, the book opens with a Table of Contents listing the grammar assumed for each story. This enables teachers to better select the appropriate material for their young translators. Next the reader will find a small glossary within each story. This glossary lists all new vocabulary words for that story not already taught in previous chapters of LFC's Primers A and B, or seen in previous stories. Within each glossary the authors have also included their own notes that fully explain those grammatical constructions unfamiliar to students. On many occasions they have also included notes pertaining to the etymology of words or their historical significance. These should provide many opportunities to further class discussions about the readings. In addition, a comprehensive glossary is included in the back, listing every word used throughout the reader. Each entry is accompanied by a reference to the chapter in which that word first appears. Lastly, readers will find a bibliography full of additional resources that may further integrate History lessons with Latin studies.

Finally, I would like to share with you my approach for both written and oral translations. This process is one I developed in my own classroom through the years; I find it to be very beneficial. Whether you choose this approach or develop one of your own, maintaining a consistent and systematic method of translating will make the experience more enjoyable for both students and teachers.

Step 1: Unfamiliar Vocabulary List

Students should make a list of all vocabulary they do not recognize or whose meaning they are uncertain of. While all vocabulary not glossed with a particular story is assumed to have already been learned or seen in previous chapters, students may have yet to seal these words in their minds. Putting this step before the actual translation may seem tedious at first. However, I guarantee that this discipline will make the translation process much smoother. Moreover, this exercise will reinforce the students' developing vocabulary and memorization skills. The more often a student must look up a given word, whose meaning eludes him, the better he will learn that word.

Step 2: Written Translation:

I generally advise that students be divided into groups of two to three for this task. Particularly in the beginning, students who have little or no experience translating passages will find some security and confidence in working together. However, I find that groups larger than three have a more difficult time collaborating effectively to obtain a good translation. Other times, you may wish to have students work independently.

When I was a child daunted by an overwhelming task, my mother would often ask, "How do you eat an elephant? One bite at a time!" (The answer that I would not ever wish to eat an elephant was never accepted). Some students may at times feel overwhelmed by the length of a passage or even a sentence. Indeed it may appear to them to be of elephantine proportions. Encourage students to tackle their elephant one sentence at a time. When compound sentences appear complex, advise students to break the sentence into smaller pieces by looking for conjunctions, commas, parentheses, quotation marks, *et cetera*.

Now that the elephant has been carved up, here's some advice on how to chew the meaty morsels and not choke on them. Latin does have a general word order (S, O, V). Its sentence structure is more loose than English, but most prose does follow certain rules. Thus, each sentence may be approached with a Question and Answer Flow which should be familiar to students of Shurley Grammar. For the passages in this reader, this simple question pattern should suffice:

1. Where is the Verb (Linking or Action)? Parse: Tense, Person, Number

2. Where is the Subject? Parse: Case, Number, Gender

3. Any Adjectives modifying the Subject? Parse: Case, Number, Gender.

4. Do we need a Direct Object, Predicate, or Indirect Object? Why? Parse: Case, Number, Gender

5. Any Adjectives modifying the D.O. /P.N. /I.O.? Parse: Case, Number, Gender.

6. Are there any Prepositions? What case does the Preposition take? Where is the Object of the Preposition? Parse: Case, Number, Gender

7. Any Adjectives modifying the O.P.? Parse: Case, Number, Gender.

8. Any word(s) left? Parse: Case, Number, Gender or Tense, Person, Number

   How does this word fit in our sentence? Why?

Repeat this process for each sentence and each subordinate clause within a sentence, and before long the elephant will be pleasantly digested!

Step 3: Oral Translation

Many classrooms may wish to end the translation process with a written exercise. While that is certainly a sufficient end for some, I feel they are missing out on a wonderful opportunity. Oral translation is my favorite part of Latin class both as a student and as a teacher. This is a wonderful exercise that has so many benefits. First, it builds great confidence in the students for they are truly reading a Latin story. Second, it works to develop oral language skills, which students will need in learning any modern language they may choose to study. Finally, oral practice helps in laying a foundation for the Rhetoric Stage, the capstone of the Trivium.

If possible, arrange students in a circle or other arrangement that enables class members to participate and interact well with one another and the teacher. Allow them their Latin passage and unfamiliar vocabulary list, but do not allow them their English translations. We all know that they can read English; this exercise is to practice reading Latin.

Before you begin reading, it is important to give everyone, including the teacher, permission to make mistakes, no matter how big they seem. No one is fluent in Latin yet. We are all learning.

One by one have students read aloud; first in Latin then in English. Longer sentences may be divided up if needed. If a student appears to be stuck, choking on a large piece of elephant, guide them through the sentence using the questions listed above. Then, ask them to re-translate the sentence smoothly on their own. Occasionally ask a student to re-translate a sentence already translated by someone else, but in a slightly different way.

Step 4: Reading Comprehension

Teaching students how to read for comprehension and specific information is an important goal at the grammar stage. It need not be limited to English grammar classes. Each story in this reader is followed by a few reading comprehension questions. They may certainly be used as a written exercise. However, I recommend asking them orally following the time of oral translation. It gives students a thrill to know they are having a Latin conversation, while at the same time exercising both their oral and reading comprehension skills. This entire translation process, from vocabulary to oral discussion, should take three class periods with a little bit of homework; possibly four periods if you prefer all work to be done in class.

Sight Translation

After orally translating a few stories as recommended above, students may be ready to take their Latin reading comprehension to a new level, Sight Translation. Try reading a story aloud to students as they silently read along. You may wish to read it to them more than once. Then ask them a few simple questions using the interrogatives they are familiar with. Use the reading comprehension questions at the bottom to guide you. The class will be amazed at how much they are able to glean from a story without first fully translating. Then walk them through the process of an oral translation. Offer as much vocabulary help as possible. The goal of this exercise is to continue to train their minds to analyze language and its grammatical structure.

As you read through these stories, be sure to take the time not only to enjoy the vocabulary and grammar contained in this little book, but the stories used to demonstrate them as well. Each one is written with a desire to capture a moment in history for these young translators, to reveal heroes of the past whose legacy is our inheritance. Do you know that John Knox was a slave aboard a French ship before bringing the Reformation to Scotland? Or that John Gutenberg made mirrors before printing the Bible? Do you know that Joan of Arc, having been executed for heresy, was acquitted just 20 years later? Many of these great events occurred while Latin was still the Lingua Franca of its day, and many of them were recorded for posterity using Rome's mother tongue. When readers reach the end of this little book, they will find one final treasure. Two ancient pieces of Latin have been included, both recorded during the time period many of these stories took place. Young translators are sure to enjoy deciphering their own Latin records of history's marvelous treasures contained in Libellus dē Historiā.

Augustinus
CCCLXXXVI A.D.

Augustinus est episcopus. Hippone habitat.

Hippo est oppidum in Africā. Augustinus multōs

librōs scrībit. Ūnus liber, <u>Confessiōnēs</u>, historiam dē

vītā Augustinī nārrat. Liber etiam fābulam dē Monicā,

mātre Augustinī, nārrat. Monica prō Augustinō multōs

annōs ōrābat.

Augustinus

GLOSSARY:

episcopus, ī, m., bishop

Hippone, abl., m., sing. = in Hippo, a city in North Africa < Hippo, Hipponis

> The names of cities use the locative case (which appears similar to the ablative) when describing place where.

Hippo, nom., m., sing. (see above)

liber, librī, m., book

scrībō, scrībere, scripsī, scriptum, to write

> This is a 3rd conjugation verb. The present tense is formed in the same way as the 1st and 2nd conjugations. Drop the –re from the infinitive and add the personal endings.

ūnus, a, um, adj., one

Confessiōnēs, nom., f., pl., Confessions

historia, ae, f., history

vīta, ae, f., life

etiam, adv., also

mātre, abl., f., sing., mother

> This is the ablative singular of the 3rd declension noun *mater*, "mother". It is here placed in the ablative case because it acts in apposition to "*Monicā.*" In Latin appositives are always placed in the same case as the noun to which they refer.

multōs annōs, accusative of duration of time = "for many years"

> This construction using the accusative case is typically used without a Latin preposition to express how long an action occurs. In English the phrase is often best translated using the preposition 'for' (i.e. "for many years").

Augustinus

Respondē Latīnē:

1. Quis est Augustinus?

2. Quis est māter Augustinī?

Quis - who

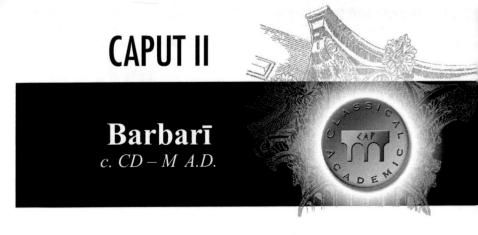

Mediō Aevō Barbarī et Northmannī magnum
imperium habent. Imperium Rōmānōrum et aliās
gentēs superant. Virī saevī et bellicōsī sunt. Capillōs
flāvōs habent. Multās terrās spoliant et vastant.

Germanī Galliam superant. Deinde Vandalī
Hispāniam superant. Deinde Visigothī Rōmam
superant. Deinde Saxonēs Brittaniam superant.

Dēnique Rōmānī et sociī Attilam Hunnum, barbarum

saevum, in Galliā superant.

Diū Northmannī oppida in lītore Europae

spoliant. Pīrātae per orbem terrārum nāvigant et

multās gentēs superant.

Post multōs annōs, Mehmet Secundus

Constantinopolem expungnat et imperium barbarōrum

superat. Hic est fīnis aevī barbarōrum.

Barbarī

GLOSSARY:

medius, a, um, adj., middle

aevum, ī, n., age, time

> Mediō Aevō, ablative of time when = in the Middle Age

This construction with the ablative is used to indicate a specific time when something occurs.

We often refer to this period of time in the plural form "the Middle Ages". The Romans, however, generally referred to a period of time in the singular form. Thus, the timer period here is in the singular "*Mediō Aevō.*"

barbarī, ōrum, m. pl., barbarians

Northmannī, ōrum, m. pl., the "Northmen" or Vikings

imperium, ī, n., power; empire

Rōmanī, ōrum, m. pl., Romans

alius, a, um, adj., other, another

gentēs, acc., pl. < gens, gentis, f., nation, tribe

superō, āre, āvī, ātum, to overcome

saevus, a, um, adj., cruel, vicious, violent, harsh

bellicōsus, a, um, adj., warlike

flāvus, a, um, adj., golden, yellow

spoliō, āre, āvī, ātum, to plunder

vastō, āre, āvī, ātum, to lay waste to, destroy, desolate

Germanī, ōrum, m. pl., Germans

Gallia, ae, f., land of the Gallī (Gauls); modern-day France

deinde, adv., then, thereupon, later

Vandalī, ōrum, m. pl., Vandals

Hispānia, ae, f., Spain

Visigothī, ōrum, m. pl., Visigoths (West Goths)

Rōma, ae, f., Rome

Saxonēs, acc., pl. < Saxo, ōnis, m., Saxon

Barbarī

Brittania, ae, f., Britain (Great Britain, including Wales & Scotland)

dēnique, adv., finally, at last

Attila Hunnus, nom., m., sing., Attila the Hun

diū, adv., for a long time

lītore, abl., sing. < lītus, lītoris, n., shore

Eurōpa, ae, f., Europe

pīrāta, ae, m., pirate, sea-robber

Like the nouns *agricola* and *nauta* this is a masculine noun of the first declension.

orbem terrārum < orbis terrārum.

Literally: "the globe of lands." But this is simply the Roman way of saying "the whole world" and so we may translate it that way.

Mehmet Secundus, nom., m., sing., Mohammed II

Constantinopolem, acc., sing< Constantinopolis, Constantinopolis, f., Constantinople

expungnō, āre, āvī, ātum, to expunge, cancel, remove

hic, nom., m., sing., pronoun, this

fīnis, nom., sing. < fīnis, fīnis, m., end

Barbarī

NOTES:
Mediō Aevō – *Ablative of Time When.* This construction with the ablative is used to indicate a specific time when something occurs.

Respondē Latīnē:

1. Quōs superant Barbarī et Northmannī?

2. Quis superat imperium barbarōrum?

Quōs – whom (accusative)
Quis – who (nominative)

CAPUT III

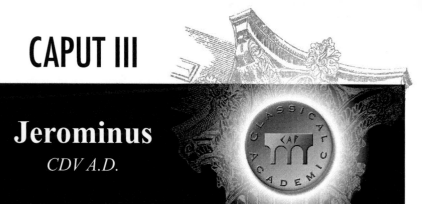

Jerominus
CDV A.D.

Jerominus erat monachus. In cavernā prope

Bethlemam habitābat. Jerominus erat vir litterātus.

Hebraeam linguam et Latīnum sciēbat. Jerominus est

clārus quod Biblia in Latīnum convertit. Haec Biblia

"Biblia Vulgāta" appellāmus, quod lingua populī vulgātī

erat Latīnum.

GLOSSARY:

monachus, ī, m., monk

caverna, ae, f., cave

Bethlema, ae, f., Bethlehem

litteratus, a, um, adj., learned, scholarly

Hebraeus, a, um, adj., Hebrew

> **Hebraeam linguam,** Literally: "the Hebrew language" or "Hebrew tongue." This phrase is used when referring to Hebrew, meaning the language.

Latīnum, ī, n., Latin (the language)

sciō, scīre, to know

> This is a 4th conjugation verb, which is not taught until much later. However, the imperfect tense is formed in a similar manner to the 1st and 2nd conjugations.

convertit, perfect tense, 3rd person, sing., = he translated

> This is the perfect tense form of the 3rd conjugation verb convertere, and is best translated with the –ed, past tense ending.

Biblia, acc., n., pl., Bible

> This noun, derived from the greek βιβλος (*biblos*) meaning book, is neuter plural in form, but translated as singular. Remember the Bible as a whole consists of several books (i.e. Genesis, Psalms, Matthew, etc.).

haec, acc., n., pl, these (neuter pronoun describing Biblia)

vulgatus, a, um, adj., common, general

Jerominus

Respondē Latīnē:

1. Quis est Jerominus?

2. Ubī habitat?

Ubī – where?
quid – what?

CAPUT IV

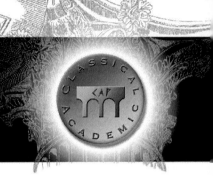

Concilium Chalcedōnis
CDLI A.D.

Post Concilium Niceano-Constantinopolitanī

erant multae falsae doctrīnae dē persōnā Christī. Multī

episcopī congregant et Dēfīnītiōnem Chalcedōnis

creant. Affirmant:

I. Christus est tōtus Deus.

II. Christus est tōtus hūmānus.

III. Christus est ūna persōna, nōn duae.

IV. Nūmen et hūmānitās Christī sunt nōn obscūrī.

Concilium Chalcedōnis

GLOSSARY:

<u>concilium</u>, ī, n., council

<u>Chalcedōnis</u>, gen., sing. < Chalcedōn, Chalcedōnis, f., Chalcedon

<u>Concilium Nicaeno-Constantinopolitanī</u> = Nicene Council

    <u>Niceano-Constantinopolitanī</u>, genitive of origin - This should be treated as one word in the genitive singular. As such the phrase, a genitive of origin, may be translated in one of two ways: Council of Nicene-Constantinople or Nicene-Constantinople Council.

<u>doctrīna</u>, ae, f., doctrine, teaching

<u>persōna</u>, ae, f., person

<u>congregō</u>, āre, āvī, ātum, to gather together, unite

<u>Dēfīnītiōnem Chalcedōnis</u> = Chalcedon Definition

    <u>Dēfīnītiōnem Chalcedōnis</u>, genitive of origin – The Definition of Chalcedon or the Chalcedon Definition.

<u>affirmō</u>, āre, āvī, ātum, to affirm

<u>tōtus</u>, a, um, adj., whole, all

<u>hūmānus</u> , a, um, adj., human

<u>ūnus</u>, a, um, adj., one

<u>duō</u>, duae, duō, adj., two

<u>nūmen</u>, nom., sing. < nūmen, nūminis, n., divine will, godhead

<u>hūmānitās</u>, nom., sing. < hūmānitās, hūmānitātis, f., human nature, humanity

<u>obscūrus</u>, a, um, adj., obscure, indistinct

Concilium Chalcedōnis

Respondē Latīnē:

1. Cūr multī episcopī cogregant?

2. Quid affirmant?

Cūr - why
quid - what

CAPUT V

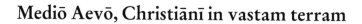

Sanctus Benedictus et Monasteria
c. DXL A.D.

Mediō Aevō, Christiānī in vastam terram

Aegyptiam movent. Christiānī virī sunt "monachī," et

Christiānae fēminae sunt "monachae." Mōx congregant.

Deinde, Sanctus Benedictus *Sanctī Benedictī*

Rēgulam parat. Litterae Benedictī monachīs multās

rēgulās dant. Sunt rēgulae dē cibō, somnō, et officiīs

dīvīnīs.

Sanctus Benedictus et Monasteria

Post occāsum Rōmae, monasteria beneficia

augent. Monachī lūdōs in monasteriīs creant. Ibi,

monachōs novōs et puerōs nobilium exercent. Dēnique,

monasteria litterās antīquās et Biblia prō posterīs

conservant.

Sanctus Benedictus et Monasteria

GLOSSARY:

sanctus, a, um, adj., holy.

> When applied to persons, this adjective can mean "saint."

Christiānus, ī, m., Christian

> Christiānus, a, um, adj., Christian

vastus, a, um, adj., desert

> vastam terram = wasteland, desert

Aegyptius, a, um, adj., Egyptian

moveō, movēre, mōvī, mōtum, to move

monacha, ae, f., nun

mox, adv., soon

rēgula, ae, f., rule

monasterium, ī, n., monastery

somnus, ī, m., sleep

officium dīvīnum = divine service

occāsum, acc., sing. < occāsus, ūs, m., fall

ibi, adv., there, then

nobilium, gen., m., pl., of the nobles

litterās, best translated as "literature" < littera, ae, f.

> In the singular this word means "letter of the alphabet." Thus, "the elements of one's education," cf. the ABC's (q.v. OLD 3). In the plural form, however, it almost always means "literature."

prō posterīs = for the sake of posterity

conservō, āre, āvī, ātum, to save, conserve

Respondē Latīnē:

1. Quī sunt *monachī?*

2. Dē quibus sunt *Rēgulae?*

3. Quās litterās conservant monasteria?

Quī – who?

Dē quibus – concerning what?

Quās - which?

CAPUT VI

Iustinianus Magnus

Imperātor Byzantiōrum,
DXXVII-DLXV A.D.

Annō DXXVII, Justinianus est imperātor

Byzantiōrum. Is est imperātor magnus. Glōriam

antīquam Rōmae commemorat. Imperium

Rōmānōrum iterum creāre labōrat.

Byzantiō Ecclēsiam "Hagiam Sophiam" (Latīnē

"sanctam sapientiam") aedificat. Aedificium est nōtum

et pulchrum.

Iustinianus Magnus

Annō DXXIX, "Cōdicem Justinianam," corpus

lēgum Rōmānārum, creat. Etiam hodiē est exemplum

lēgibus multārum gentium.

Iustinianus Magnus

GLOSSARY:

<u>annō</u>, ablative of time within which = in the year...

<u>Justinianus, ī</u>, m., Justinian

<u>imperātor, imperātōris</u>, m., commander, leader; emperor

<u>Byzantius, ī</u>, m., Byzantine

<u>iterum</u>, adv., again

<u>labōrō + inf.</u> = to pains, work for, work to . . .

<u>Byzantiō</u>, = in Byzantium

    Byzantium is the city known as Constantinople, modern day Istanbul. The names of cities use the locative case (which appears similar to the ablative) when describing place where.

<u>ecclēsia, ae</u>, f., church

<u>Hagia Sophia</u>, f., Greek for "Holy Wisdom"

<u>Latīnē</u>, adv., in Latin

<u>sapientia, ae</u>, f., wisdom

<u>aedificō, āre, āvī, ātum</u>, to build.

    cf. aedificium, ī, n., building, structure.

<u>cōdicem</u>, acc., sing.< cōdex, cōdicis, f., book

    The older spelling of the word is caudex. The original meaning of the word is "trunk of stem of a tree." It comes to mean a book which is made of wooden covers (q.v. OLD 1, 2).

<u>Justinianus, a, um</u>, adj., of or pertaining to Justinian

<u>corpus</u>, acc., sing.< corpus, corporis, n., body; collection

<u>lēgum</u>, gen., pl.< lex, lēgis, f., law

<u>hodiē</u>, adv., today

<u>lēgibus</u>, dat., pl.< lex, lēgis (see above)

    Remember that the dative can be translated with the preposition "for." Here, the syntax is a dative of reference or advantage. See AG 376.

<u>gentium</u>, gen., pl.< gens, gentis, f., clan; nation

Iustinianus Magnus

Respondē Latīnē:

1. Quid appellāmus Hagiam Sophiam Latīnē?

2. Quae creat Justinianus?

quid – what?
quae – which things?

CAPUT VII

Muhammed et Religio Islamica

DLXX - DCXXXII A.D.

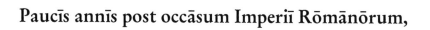

Paucīs annīs post occāsum Imperiī Rōmānōrum,

Muhammed, auctor religiōnis Islamicae, in vastam

terram Arabicam it. Multīs somnium Angelī Gabrielis

nūntiat. Paucī verba crēdunt; multī rident. Mox eī

insidiās dant. Muhammed cum uxōre Medinam fugit.

Fuga Medinam incipium fastōrum Islamicōrum est.

Muhammed et Religio Islamica

Religiō Muhammedis quīnque praecepta habet.

Sectatōrēs praeceptīs parēre dēbent. Praecepta Islamica

in Al-Coranō sunt. Al-Coranus est scriptūra Islamicae.

Sectatōrēs Muhammedis in Asiam, Africam, et

Hispāniam eunt.

Muhammed et Religio Islamica

GLOSSARY:

paucī, paucae, pauca, adj., (always plural), a few

    paucīs annīs, ablative of time within which = "in a few years"

occāsum, acc., sing.< occāsus, ūs, m., collapse, fall

Muhammed, Muhammedis, m., Mohammed

    Muhammedis, gen., sing., of Mohammed

auctor, nom., sing. < auctor, auctōris, m., author, founder

religiōnis, gen., sing. < religiōnis, religiōnis, f., religion

Islamicus, a, um, adj., Islamic

Arabicus, a, um, adj., Arabian, Arabic

somnium, ī, n., dream, vision

angelus, ī, m., angel

Gabrielis, gen., sing. < Gabriel, Gabrielis, m., Gabriel

nūntiō, āre, āvī, ātum, announce, report

crēdō, crēdere, to believe

    This verb takes an accusative for the thing believed, but a dative for the person believed in.

rideō, ridēre, rīsī, rīsum, to laugh

insidiae, ārum, f.pl., plots, conspiracy

uxōre, abl., sing. < uxor, uxōris, f., wife

Medinam, accusative of place to which = to Medina < Medina, ae, f.

    The names of cities use the accusative case without a preposition to express motion towards.

fuga, fugae, f., flight, escape

incipium, ī, n., beginning

fastī, fastōrum, m.pl., calendar

    This noun is plural in form, but singular in meaning. Think of a calendar as a list of dates.

Muhammed et Religio Islamica

praeceptum, ī, n., teaching, rule, principle

sectatōrēs, nom., pl.< sectator, sectatōris, m., follower

parēre + infinitive = "to obey" < pareō, parēre, obey.

      This verb takes a dative of the thing/person obeyed instead of an accusative direct object.

dēbeō, dēbēre, dēbuī, dēbitum, owe, ought (usually with an infinitive)

Al-Coranus, ī, m., the Koran

Asia, ae, f., the Near East

Africa, ae, f., Africa

Muhammed et Religio Islamica

Respondē Latīnē:

1. Quī est auctor religiōnis Islamicae?

2. Quod est sciptūra Islamicae?

quī – who?

quod – what?

CAPUT VIII

Carolus Magnus
DCCXLII – DCCCXIV A.D.

Carolus rēx magnus est. Ergō nōs vocāmus

Carolum "Magnum." Pontifex Leo III eī corōnam

Imperiī Rōmānī dat. Carolus est mīles bonus. Lēgēs,

cīvitātem, et doctrīnam Christiānam per Eurōpam

auget. Magnam partem Eurōpae regit.

Carolus Magnus

Carolus rēx bonus est. Scholās monachōrum

auget. Per auctoritātem eius, scholae litterās Graecās

et Rōmānās conservant. Scriptūrās Sacrās prō posterīs

conservant.

Carolus Magnus

GLOSSARY:

<u>Carolus</u>, ī, m., Charles

<u>rēx</u>, nom., sing. < rēx, rēgis, m., king

<u>ergo</u>, adv. conj., therefore

<u>Pontifex</u>, nom., sing.< Pontifex, Pontificis, m., Pope

This word was used by the Romans for a priest, particularly the *Pontifex Maximus* or high priest of Rome, a position of great power and authority. The title was adopted by the Catholic Church also to mean the high priest of Rome, the supreme head of the Roman Catholic Church.

<u>eī</u> dat., m., sing., to him < is, ea, id

The dative case is used for indirect objects and is often translated with the English prepositions "to" or "for." However these prepositions are not always necessary and may be omitted. i.e., *eī corōnam dat* = he gives the crown to him; he gives him the crown

<u>corōna</u>, ae, f., wreath, crown

<u>mīles</u>, nom., sing. < mīles, mīlitis, m., soldier

<u>lēgēs</u>, acc., pl. < lex, lēgis, f., law

<u>cīvitātem</u>, acc., sing., < cīvitās, cīvitātis, f., civilization, civilized society

<u>partem</u>, acc., sing.< pars, partis, f., part

<u>regō, regere</u>, to rule, govern

<u>schola</u>, ae, f., school

This refers to an advanced school, not a primary or grammar school, which was called a *lūdus*.

<u>auctoritātem</u>, acc., sing. < auctoritās, auctoritātis, f., authority, power

<u>litterās</u>, best translated as "literature" < littera, ae, f.

See note regarding *litterae* in Chapter 5, **Sanctus Benedictus et Monasteria**

<u>Graecus, a, um</u>, adj., Greek

<u>sacer, sacra, sacrum</u>, adj., holy, sacred

Carolus Magnus

Respondē Latīnē:

1. Quī dat Carolō corōnam?

2. Quae servant scholae?

quī – who?

quae – what things?

CAPUT IX

Aelfredus Magnus
Rex Angulsaxōnum,
DCCCLXXI-CMI A.D.

Aelfredus Magnus est rēx Occidentalium Saxōnum.

Annō DCCCLXV exercitus pāgānōrum Danicōrum

Brittaniam oppugnat. Annō DCCCLXXVIII Aelfredus

pāgānōs superat. Dēnique, pācem cum Angulsaxōnibus

meridianae Brittaniae pangit.

Aelfredus litterās et doctrīnam Christiānam

ex excidiō pāgānōrum Danicōrum conservat. Lūdōs

Aelfredus Magnus

fundat. Aelfredus est vir litterātus. In librīs et lēgibus,

fīdem Christiānam inter Angulsaxōnēs augēre labōrat.

Aelfredus Magnus

GLOSSARY:

Nota Bene: The specialized vocabulary for this story is largely based on the ninth century biography of Alfred, <u>Life of Alfred</u>, by the monk Asser.

<u>Aelfredus</u>, ī, m. Alfred

<u>rēx</u>, nom., sing.< rēx, rēgis, m., king

<u>Angulsaxōnum</u>, gen., pl. < Angulsaxon, Angulsaxōnis, m., Anglo-Saxon

<u>Occidentalium</u>, gen., m., pl. < Occidental, Occidentalis, adj., Western

> N.B. - The southern English district of Wessex comes from the combination of the words "West" and "Saxon."

<u>Saxōnum</u>, gen., pl. < Saxon, Saxōnis, m., Saxon

<u>annō</u>, ablative of time within which = in the year...

<u>exercitus</u>, ūs, m., army

> This is a 4th declension noun, but it looks like a 2nd declension noun in the nominative and accusative singular.

<u>pāgānus</u>, ī, m., belonging to a village, rural; here, "pagans," as opposed to Christians.

> Asser calls the Danish Vikings simply *pāgānī*, without a specific reference to their ethnicity. The word *pāgānus*, originating from *pāgus*, village or district, simply denoted a non-urban person or thing. It could also mean "civilian," as opposed to military. In the Christian period, the word comes to mean "non-Christian," as those who lived in the hinterlands were more likely to be unevangelized (cf. the etymology of *heathen*). Asser is mainly concerned with contrasting the spiritual state of the Danes with that of the *Christiānī*, that is, the Anglo-Saxons. For clarity's sake, the epithet *Danicī* has been supplied. In classical prose, the idea of "raiders" or "sackers" could have been expressed with *pīrāta*.

<u>pācem</u>, acc., sing. < pax, pācis, f., peace

<u>Angulsaxōnibus</u>, abl., m., pl. (see above)

Aelfredus Magnus

Merīdiānus, a, um, adj., Southerly, Southern
pangō, pangere, to fasten; settle
excidium, ī, n., destruction
lēgibus, abl., pl. < lex, lēgis, f., law
fidem, acc., sing.< fidēs, ēī, f., faith

Respondē Latīnē:

1. Quī oppugnat Brittaniam?

2. Quae conservat Aelfredus?

quī – who

quae – which things

CAPUT X

Otto I et Imperium Rōmānum
XCLXII - XCLXXIII A.D.

Multōs annōs post mortem Carolī Magnī, Otto I

Rēx Germanōrum est. Otto I rēx fortis est. Multōs

ducēs subiungit. Deinde etiam Rēx Ītalōrum est.

Eō tempore Ecclēsia Rōmāna serva ducum

profānōrum est. Ducēs pontificibus officium dant. Sīc

officium pontificis nōn firmum est.

Otto I et Imperium Rōmānum

Propter opēs Ottōnis, Pontifex Iohannes XII

auxilium rogat. Prō hōc bonō, Pontifex eum appellat

Imperātōrem Rōmānōrum. Otto gentēs Eurōpae

conciliat. Eurōpam sub imperium Germanōrum

subiungit.

Otto I et Imperium Rōmānum

GLOSSARY:

<u>Otto</u>, nom., sing.< Otto, Ottōnis, m., Otto

<u>multōs annōs</u>, accusative of duration of time = during the many years . . .

<u>mortem</u>, acc., sing.< mors, mortis, f., death

> <u>post mortem</u>, literally: after death – This is a phrase still used commonly today amongst the medical community. Not to be confused with p.m. or *post meridiem* (after noon).

<u>Carolus Magnus</u>, m., Charles the Great ("Charlemagne")

<u>Germanī, ōrum</u>, m. pl., Germans

<u>rēx</u>, nom., sing. < rēx, rēgis, m., king

<u>fortis</u>, adj. modifying rēx, brave, strong

<u>ducēs</u>, acc., pl.,< dux, ducis, m., leader

<u>subiungō, subiungere, subiunxī, subiunctum</u>, harness; bring under the control of, subjugate

<u>Ītalī, ōrum</u>, m. pl., Italians

<u>eō tempore</u>, ablative of time within which = in that time

> *Eō* may be recognized as the ablative masculine/neuter singular form of the 3rd person personal pronoun *is, ea, id* recently learned in chapter 6 of LFC, B. This pronoun may also serve as a demonstrative adjective translated as "that". i.e. - eō *tempore* = at that time. Other demonstrative pronoun/adjectives will be introduced in chapters 22 – 24 of LFC, B.

<u>ducum</u>, gen., pl.< dux, ducis (see above)

<u>profānus, a, um</u>, adj., secular, not religious

<u>pontificibus</u>, dat., pl. < Pontifex, ficis, m., Pope

Remember, the dative case may be translated using the prepositions "to" or "for."

See note regarding the *Pontifex Maximus* in chapter 8, **Carolus Magnus**.

<u>Iohannes, is</u>, m., John

Otto I et Imperium Rōmānum

sīc, adv., thus

firmus, a, um, adj., steady, secure

propter, prep. + acc., on account of, because of

opēs, acc., f., pl., wealth, resources, military resources < opēs, opum

> This word, when used in the plural form, refers to wealth or military resources. Think of wealth (a singular word) as an accumulation of many (plural) resources and much money.

Ottōnis, gen., sing. < Otto (see above)

prō hōc bonō = for this good thing/deed (benefit)

imperātorem, acc., sing. < imperātor, imperātōris, m., commander, emperor

> eum appellat Imperātorem, *Imperātorem* is a predicate accusative, "calls him Emperor . . . "

gentēs, acc., pl. < gens, gentis, f. tribe, nation

conciliō, āre, āvī, ātum, to unite, bring together

sub, prep. + acc., up under, beneath

> This preposition, though commonly used with the ablative to mean "under," may also take the accusative case to mean "up under, beneath." The uses of *sub* and other prepositions will be reviewed in the succeeding chapters 11 & 12 of LFC, B.

Otto I et Imperium Rōmānum

Respondē Latīnē:

1. Quis est Otto?

2. Quid Ottōnem Iohannes appellat?

quis – who?
quid – what?

CAPUT XI

Schisma Orientalis Ecclēsiae Occidentalisque Ecclēsiae
MLIV A.D.

Contrōversia dē Spīritō Sanctō erat magna causa

schismae intrā Ecclēsiam Christianam. Orientalis

Ecclēsia Spīritum Sanctum prōcēdere ex Patre sōlō

putābat. Occidentalis Ecclēsia autem Spīritum

Sanctum prōcēdere ex Patre Fīliōque putābat. Ubī

Occidentalis Ecclēsia novum verbum, "Fīliōque," in

Symbolum Nicaeno-Constantinopolitanum adoptat,

Orientalem Ecclēsiam nōn rogant. Orientalis Ecclēsia

est īrāta. Propter contrōversiam, Ecclēsia Christiana

in Rōmānam Catholicam Ecclēsiam et Orientalem

Ecclēsiam separābit.

GLOSSARY:

contrōversia, ae, f., controversy, argument

schisma, ae, f., schism

Orientalis, adjective modifying *ecclēsia*, Eastern

prōcēdō, prōcēdere, to proceed

putābat Spīritum Sanctum prōcēdere, Indirect Discourse, literally translated, "the church thinks the Holy Spirit to proceed . . . "

When describing what someone is thinking or saying in English the preposition 'that' is commonly used: "The church thinks that the Holy Spirit proceeds." When describing the same Indirect Discourse in Latin, an accusative + infinitive is used.

Patre, abl., sing. < pater, patris, m., father

sōlus, a, um, adj., only, alone

Occidentalis, adjective modifying *ecclēsia*, Western

Orientalis, Occidentalis, 3rd declension adjectives - The *-is* ending may be either nominative or genitive singular depending on the context of the sentence. *Occidentalis* appeared previously in chapter 9, **Aelfredus Magnus.**

autem, conjunction, on the other hand, however, but

Fīliōque =Fīliō+ que (and)

The suffix, *-que,* is an enclitic. Enclitics are words which do not stand on their own but attach themselves to the end of the following word. An example of an enclitic in English would be the conjunction 'n'. (i.e. – bacon 'n' eggs, salt 'n' pepper)

ubī, adv., when

Symbolum Nicaeno-Constantinopolitanum = Nicene Symbol or Nicene Creed

The longer more formal name refers to the second ecumenical Council, which was convened by Theodosius in Constantinople, to which the origin of this document has been traced. The Council consisted of 150 bishops, all from the East.

separō, āre, āvī, ātum, to separate, divide

Respondē Latīnē:

1. Quid est causa schismae?

2. Quid novum verbum Occidentalis Ecclēsia adoptat?

3. Cūr Orientalis Ecclēsia est īrāta?

quid – what
cūr - why

CAPUT XII

Līberī in Mediō Aevō
c. M – MCD A.D.

In Mediō Aevō, paene nullī līberī ad lūdum eunt.

Saepe līberī in agrīs labōrant, aut parvōs germānōs et

parvās germānās cūrant. Familiae dīvitiārum interdum

līberōs monasteriō dant. Illī līberī erunt monachī et

monachae. Monachī līberōs legere et scrībere docent.

Familiae maximārum dīvitiārum interdum magistrum

in casā habent. Visne habitāre in Mediō Aevō?

Līberī in Mediō Aevō

GLOSSARY

In Mediō Aevō, ablative of time = In the Middle Age

The ablative case is used to indicate the time when something occurs. The ablative of time is often used without a preposition, but may include a preposition for emphasis. The preposition in has been used here since the students are reviewing those prepositions which take the ablative case.

paene, adv., almost

līberī, liberōrum, m. pl., children

This noun is only used in the plural form. It is derived from the verb *līberāre*, to *free*, because children were seen as little people *free from* the burdens of responsibility that come with age.

saepe, adv., often

aut, conj., or

cūrō, āre, āvī, ātum, to care for

dīvitiae, dīvitiārum, f. pl., wealth

This noun is only used in its plural form. Think of wealth as riches, or lots of money/possessions. This plural noun may be compared to *opēs* used in chapter 10, **Otto I et Imperium Rōmānam**. The 2nd declension *dīvitiae* is used with strict reference to money and material wealth, whereas the 3rd declension *opēs* is used to express wealth in terms not only of money, but power and military might.

interdum, adv., sometimes

illī, nom., m., pl., those <ille, illa, illud, demonstrative pronoun, that, those

The demonstrative pronoun ille will be taught in chapter 23 of LFC, B.

legō, legere, to read

doceō, docēre, docuī, doctum, to teach

maximus, a, um, superlative adj., greatest

visne = (vis + ne) do you wish?

Līberī in Mediō Aevō

Like the *–que* of *Fīliōque* in the previous story, *-ne* is an enclitic. The enclitic *-ne* signals the asking of a yes/no question. *Vis* is the second person singular form of the irregular verb *volō*, *velle*, *to wish*. For further explanation concerning enclitics, see chapter 11, **Schisma Orientalis Ecclēsiae Occidentalisque Ecclēsiae.**

Respondē Latīnē:

1. **Ubī multī līberī labōrant?**

2. **Quis līberōs ē familiīs dīvitiārum docet?**

3. **Visne habitāre in Mediō Aevō?**

Ubī – Where?

Quis – Who?

Minime – no!

ita vero – yes!

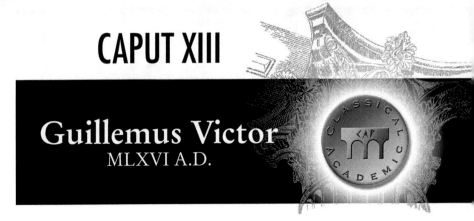

Guillemus Victor
MLXVI A.D.

Guillemus est dux Normannōrum. Sed avet

esse Rēx Anglōrum.   Angliōs oppugnat. In Proeliō

Hastingae Haroldum, prīncipem Anglōrum, superat.

Guillemus iam est Rēx Anglōrum, sed modo Dux

Normannōrum. Proptereā diū rēgēs Anglōrum augēre

terrās in Galliā avent.

Guillemus Victor

GLOSSARY:

Guillemus, Guillemī, m., William

victor, nom., sing. < victor, victoris, m., conquerer

dux, nom., sing.< dux, ducis, m., leader; duke, prince

This word literally means "leader, ruler, commander." Our word *duke* (a prince who rules a duchy) is derived from this Latin noun. Therefore *dux* best fits the Latin equivalent for this title of nobility.

Normannī, Normannōrum, m.pl., Normans

aveō, avēre, (+infinitive) to want eagerly

avet esse = he wants to be

Anglī, Anglōrum, m.pl., the English

Haroldus, Haroldī, m., Harold

Hastinga, Hastingae, f., Hastings

prīncipem, acc., sing.< prīncips, prīncipis, m/f., prince, leader

iam, adv., now, already

proptereā adv., on account of this

rēgēs, acc., pl.< rēx, rēgis, m., king

modo, adv., only

Guillemus Victor

Respondē Latīnē:

1. Quem Guillemus superat in Proeliō Hastingae?

2. Quis est Haroldus?

quem – whom? (accusative)
quis- who? (nominative)

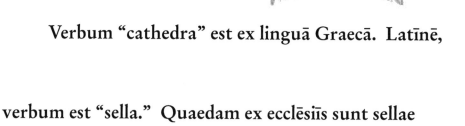

Cathedralēs in Eurōpā
c. MC A.D.

Verbum "cathedra" est ex linguā Graecā. Latīnē,

verbum est "sella." Quaedam ex ecclēsiīs sunt sellae

auctōritātis episcopōrum. Appellant eās "cathedralēs."

Iam diū aedificia ecclēsiārum erant generis

Rōmānī. Circā annum MC, genus novum aedificiōrum

appāret. Quod genus est ex Eurōpā Aquilōnariā, Ītalī

appellant id "Gothicum."

Cathedralēs in Eurōpā

Aedificāre cathedralem erat difficile et cārum.

Artificēs ūnum cathedralem multōs annōs aedificāre

labōrābant. Ecclēsia Rōmāna populum multam

pecūniam petebat e populī. Sed aedificia sunt pulchra

exempla artis hūmānae prō glōriā Deī.

Cathedralēs in Eurōpā

GLOSSARY:

cathedra, This Latin word is derived from the Greek word **καθέδρα** (chair).

sella, ae, f., seat, chair

quaedam ex ecclēsiīs = certain churches, some churches

Literally translated as, "certain ones out of the churches." The pronoun *quaedam*, like most numerals, is commonly followed by the preposition ex + ablative instead of the partitive genitive in order to indicate a part of the whole. The use of the ablative and genitive with numbers will be discussed more thoroughly in chapter 17 of LFC, B. (also see *AG* 346c)

auctōritātis, gen., sing., < auctōritās, auctōritātis, f., authority

appellant, Latin, like English, uses indefinite subjects with some verbs of saying, speaking, or telling. e.g., "*They* call this place Dead Man's curve." (See AG 318b)

cathedralēs, acc., f., pl.< cathedralis, e, adj., cathedral (understand "ecclēsiās.")

The adjective "*cathedralis*" means "of or pertaining to a bishop's see." The noun "*ecclēsia*" is understood but not expressed.

generis, gen., sing.,< genus, generis, n., origin; kind, fashion

appāreō, appārēre, appāruī, appāritum, to become visible, appear

Aquilōnarius, a, um, adj., Northern

Gothicus, a, um, adj., Gothic

cathedralem, acc., f., sing. < cathedralis (see above)

est difficile = It is difficult...

This construction, namely that of a neuter predicate adjective with an infinitive subject, is very common. In grammatical terms, the subject of the sentence is actually the infinitive, which is a verbal noun, neuter in gender. (See *AG* 452)

cārus, a, um, adj., dear, expensive

Cathedralēs in Eurōpā

<u>multōs annōs</u>, accusative of duration of time = for many years...

The syntax of this phrase is "accusative of duration of time." The accusative shows the extent of time over which an action takes place, as opposed to the ablative, which can show the "time within which" an action took place.

<u>artificēs</u>, nom., pl.< artifex, artifices, m., craftsman, artisan

<u>petō, petere, petīvī, petītum</u>, to seek, aim at, beg

<u>pecūnia, ae</u>, f., money

<u>artis</u>, gen., sing.< ars, artis, f., skill, art (cf. artifex above)

Respondē Latīnē:

1. Quid significat "cathedra" in Latīnē?

2. Quid Ītalī novum aedificium ex Eurōpā Aquilōnariā appellant?

quid significat – what does it mean?
quid – what?

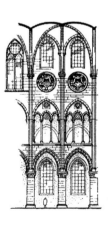

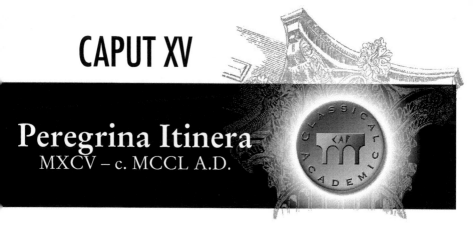

CAPUT XV

Peregrina Itinera
MXCV – c. MCCL A.D.

Pontifex Urbanus populum occupāre

Hierosolymōs ab Islamicīs suādet. Populus clāmat

"Deus vult!" Multī sunt parātī. Propter multās causās

eunt ad Terram Sanctam.

In Peregrinō Itinerō Prīmō Hierosolymōs

occupant. Sed in peregrinīs itinerīs posterīs victōriam

nōn habent. In tōtō sunt octō peregrina itinera.

Peregrina Itinera

GLOSSARY:

<u>Pontifex</u>, nom., sing. < Pontifex, Pontificis, m., Pope

See note regarding the *Pontifex Maximus* in chapter 8, **Carolus Magnus**.

<u>Urbanus, Urbanī, m.,</u> Urban

<u>occupō, āre, āvī, ātum,</u> to seize, attack

<u>Hierosolyma, ōrum, m. pl.,</u> Jerusalem

<u>suādeō, suādēre, suāsī, suāsum,</u> to suggest; urge

<u>vult</u>, irregular verb = he wants, wishes < volō, velle

<u>peregrinum iter</u>, n., crusade, pilgrimage < peregrinum, adj. + iter, itineris, n.

      Literally the phrase may be translated as "foreign journey."

<u>posterus, postera, posterum,</u> adj. the following, the future

<u>in tōtō</u> = in all, in total

Respondē Latīnē:

1. Quid clāmat populus?

2. Quot peregrina itinera sunt?

3. Quot victoriās habent?

quid – what?
quot – how many?

CAPUT XVI

Sanctus Franciscus Assisiensis

MCLXXXII - MCCXXIV A.D.

Sanctus Franciscus Assisiensis erat adulēscēns

malus. Post morbum malum, ad Christianitātem

convertit. Familia eius dīvitiās habet, sed Franciscus

pecūniam et bona semper dat, sīcut Christus iubet.

Dēnique, familia eius eum dimittit et Franciscus in silvā

habitat.

Sanctus Franciscus Assisiensis

Deinde, exemplō Christī paret; et paupertātem

exercet et dē eā adnūntiat. Assisiem redit. Quīdam cum

eō congregant.

Franciscus dē imitatiōne Christī adnūntiat. Et

Franciscus et discipulī, "Frātrēs Minōrēs," sine pecūnia

labōrant. Annō MCCXXIII, Pontifex Honorius

congregatiōnem probat et eam "ordinem" appellat.

Post mortem Franciscī, Frātrēs Minōrēs per terram

adnūntiat.

Sanctus Franciscus Assisiensis

GLOSSARY:

Francsicus Assisiensis = Francis of Assisi

adulēscēns, nom., sing.< adulēscēns, adulēscentis, m/f., youth

morbus, ī, m., sickness, illness

Christianitātem, acc., sing.< Christianitās, Christianitātis, f., Christianity

convertō, convertere, to turn round; turn, direct.

bona, acc., n., pl., < bonus, a, um.

Here, the adjective is used as a noun, meaning literally "goods."
This is referred to as a "substantive adjective." That is an adjective
that *stands (cf. stō, stāre)* in the place of a noun. Just as in English,
one's "goods" are one's possessions.

semper, adv., always

sīcut, adv., just as

Christus, ī, m., Christ

dimittō, dimittere, to send forth, send away

pareō, ēre, (+ dative) to obey. This is literally translated as "to be
obedient to..." Some verbs, such as *parēre*, take an object in the
dative case instead of the accusative.

i.e.: *exemplō Christī paret* = he obeys the example of Christ
See also the note regarding this same verb in chapter 7.

et . . . et = both . . . and

paupertātem, acc., sing. < paupertās, paupertātis, f., poverty

exerceō, besides "train" can also mean "practice."
In addition to meaning "to train" *exercēre* may also be translated as
"to practice." After all, to train is to practice repeatedly. This same
usage can be seen in chapter 5, **Sanctus Benedictus et Monasteria.**

adnūntiō, āre, āvī, ātum, to proclaim, preach

adnūntiāre = ad + nūntiāre, This compound verb would literally mean
" to announce to" an audience. This comes to mean "proclaim, preach."

Sanctus Franciscus Assisiensis

<u>Frātrēs Minōrēs</u>, "lesser brothers," the official Latin name of the Franciscan order.

<u>Assisiem</u> = to Assisi < Assisis, is, f. Assisi

> The names of cities use the accusative without a preposition to express motion towards.

<u>redeō, īre</u>, to return, go back

<u>quīdam</u>, nominative pronoun, certain ones

<u>imitatiōne</u>, abl., sing.< imitātiō, imitātiōnis, f., imitation

<u>Pontifex</u>, nom., sing.< Pontifex, Pontificis, m., Pope

> See the note regarding the *Pontifex Maximus* in chapter 8, Carolus Magnus.

<u>congregatiōnem</u>, acc., sing. congregātiō, congregātiōnis, f., congregation, group

<u>probō, āre, āvī, ātum</u>, to approve (of)

<u>ordinem</u>, acc., sing.,< ordō, ordinis, m., order

<u>mortem</u>, acc., sing.< mors, mortis, f., death

Respondē Latīnē:

1. Quandō Franciscus convertit?

2. Ubī Franciscus habitat? Cūr?

3. Ubī Frātrēs Minōrēs adnūntiat?

quandō – When?
ubī – Where?
cūr? – Why?

Magna Carta
MCCXV A.D.

Iohannes, germānus Ricardī, erat malus rēx. Erat

ōn iūstus. Multōs vectigalēs impōnēbat. Sic, quintō

ecimō diē Iuniī, annō MCCXV, vīgintī quinque baronēs

um obsignāre Magnam Cartam cōgunt. Magna Carta

st prīma litterārum quae potestātem rēgis terminābunt.

GLOSSARY:

Ricardus, ī, m., Richard

rēx, nom., sing.< rēx, rēgis, m., king

vectigalēs, acc., pl.< vectigal, vectigalis m., tax

impōnō, impōnere, to impose

diē, ablative of time when = on the ___th day < diēs, dieī, m., day

> This construction with the ablative is used to indicate a specific time when something occurs.

Iunius, ī, m., June

annō, ablative of time within which = in the year . . .

> This construction with the ablative is similar to that of 'time when.' It indicates a broader space of time within which something occurs.

baronēs, nom., pl. < baro, baronis, m., barons

obsignō, āre, āvī, ātum, to sign

cōgō, cōgere, to force

litterārum, best translated here as 'documents'

> See note regarding the translation of *litterae* in chapter 5, Sanctus Benedictus et Monasteria.

quae, relative pronoun referring to litterae = which

potestātem, acc., sing. < potestās, potestātis, f., power

rēgis, gen. sing. < rēx (see above)

terminō, āre, āvī, ātum, to limit

Magna Carta

NOTA BENE:

quintō decimō diē Iuniī – This date appears in accordance with our modern calendar. The Roman calendar would have dated this event in history as ***a.d. XVII Kalendās Iuliās*** (seventeen days before the Kalends of July). The Romans had three regular holidays each month. The Kalends fell on the first day, the Nones on the fifth or seventh, and the Ides on the thirteenth or fifteenth. The Romans counted down to each of these holidays much like we count down to Christmas.

Respondē Latīnē:

1. Quis est Iohannes?

2. Quid obsignat?

3. Quandō Iohannes Magnam Cartam obsignat?

quis – who?
quid – what?
quandō – when?

CAPUT XVIII

Thoma Aquinas
MCCXXV – MCCLXXIV A.D.

Thoma, nātus annō dominī MCCXXV in familiam

dīvitiārum, in Hispāniā habitat. Quinque annōs nātus,

cum monachīs Benedictī habitat. Monachī eum docent.

Monachī lūdum habent et eī multōs puerōs docent.

Thoma discere amat. Saepe, eōs rogat, "Quid est Deus?"

Thoma Aquinas

Olim parvus Thoma erit monachus Dominicanus.

Multī virī, etiam Pontifex, sapientiam eius quaerent.

Thoma erit notus propter magnum opus, <u>Summam</u>

<u>Theologicam.</u>

GLOSSARY:

Thoma, ae, m., Thomas

quinque annōs nātus, This is a classical idiom used to express one's age. Literally translate as, "having been born five years." It may also be translated as the English expression, "when he is five years old."

discō, discere, to learn

quid, interrogative pronoun = what

olim, adv., someday

Dominicanus, a, um, adj., Dominican

Pontifex, nom., sing. < Pontifex, Pontificis, m., Pope

See note regarding the *Pontifex Maximus* in chapter 8, **Carolus Magnus.**

quaerent, future, 3rd person, pl. = they will seek < quaerō, quaerere, to seek

opus, operis, n., work

magnum opus = great work

This phrase usually refers to someone's greatest achievement. *Opus* alone is often used to describe not only literary works, but also music:

Mozart's Opus 4, consisting of three concertos, was published in 1785. (Piano concerto no. 11 in F major, Piano concerto no. 13 in C major, Piano concerto no. 12 in A major)

Thoma Aquinas

NOTA BENE:

Thomas Aquinas's *magnum opus*, <u>Summa Theologica</u>, was written in Latin just as his other works. His approach to writing was a very orderly one. <u>Summa Theologica</u> was divided into three main parts. Each part was then further divided into numbered questions. Each question was divided once again into articles to be addressed by the author.

Respondē Latīnē:

1. Ubī Thoma habitābat?

2. Quid est magnum opus eius?

quandō - when?
ubī - where?
quid - what?

CAPUT XIX

Marcus Polo
MCCLIV - MCCCXXIV A.D.

Marcus Polo est fīlius mercātoris Venetiānī. Cum

patre et patruō ad regnum Sinārum it. Imperātor

Sinārum Ītaliīs favet. In aulā imperātōris diū habitant.

Cum Marcus Polo ad Ītaliam redit, librum dē peregrinīs

scrībit.

Marcus Polo

GLOSSARY:

Marcus Polo, nom., m., sing., Marco Polo

mercātor, mercātoris, m., merchant

Venetianus, a, um, adj., Venetian

patruus, patruī, m., uncle (on the father's side)

The Romans differentiated between aunts & uncles on the father's side and those on the mother's side.

patruus – paternal uncle	*avunculus* – maternal uncle
amita - paternal aunt	*mātertera* – maternal aunt

Sina, Sinae, m., Chinese

Ītalī, Ītalōrum, m.pl., Italians

faveō, favēre, fāvī, fautum, (+ dative) to favor.

Some verbs such as *favēre* take an object in the dative case instead of the accusatiave.

aula, aulae, f., court

diū, adv., for a long time

cum, adverbial conjunction, when

redeō, redīre, rediī, redītum, to return (compound of re + eō)

Marcus Polo

Respondē Latīnē:

1. Quō Marcus it?

2. Quibuscum ad Regnum Sinārum it?

quō – where? to what place?
quibuscum – with whom?

Nota Bene:

Quibuscum = *Quibus* (interrogative pronoun) + *cum* (enclitic) = with whom?

Students may recognize the ending *–ibus* on this interrogative pronoun as the ablative plural of the 3rd declension. The familiar preposition *cum*, which takes the ablative case, is acting here as an enclitic. See note regarding enclitics in chapter 11.

CAPUT XX

Joanna Darco
MCDXII – MCDXXXI A.D.

Tricesimō diē Maiae, annō MCDXXXI, Iūdicium

Brittaniae Rotomagō (urbe in Galliā) Ioannam Darco

damnāvit. Adulēscentem propter haeresem igne

necāvit. Annō MCDXLIX, dēnique Gallī Britannicōs

Rotomagō expungant. Gallica Inquīsītiō iam novum

iūdicium prō Ioannā incipit. Quaesitor testēs interrogat

et documenta perscrūtat. Deinde, septimō diē Iuliī,

Joanna Darco

annō MCDLVI, Quaesitor Ioannam innocentem

et martyrem dēclārat. Nam prīmum iūdicium erat

fraudulentum et illicitum.

Joanna Darco

GLOSSARY:

<u>tricesimō diē</u>, ablative of time = on the thirtieth day

<u>Maia, ae,</u> f., May

<u>iūdicium, iūdiciī,</u> n., court

<u>Ioanna Darco</u> (Joanna Darco) nom., f., sing., Joan of Arc

    Joanna is the Latinization of the common name Joan or Jeanne, as the martyr signed her name to her last letter to Rheims on March 28, 1430. The Latin *Darco* comes from the Medieval "Darc" instead of d'Arc, as there was a lack of apostrophes in the 15th century. There is still a great deal of speculation as to whether "Darc" refers to a specific location or perhaps a family surname.

<u>damnāvit</u> - 3rd person sing., perfect tense = it condemned < damnō, āre

<u>Rotomagō</u> = in Rouen; from Rouen < Rotomagus, ī, m., Rouen

    Prepositions are neither used to express place where nor place from which. Use the context clues to decipher which translation is most appropriate for each usage.

<u>urbe,</u> This noun is operating in apposition to *Rotomagō*. Appositives are placed in the same case as the noun to which they refer.

<u>haeresis, haeresis,</u> f., heresy, sect, school of thought

<u>ignis, ignis,</u> m. (i-stem), fire

    <u>igne</u>, ablative of instrument. The ablative case is often used without a preposition to indicate the means or instrument used to accomplish an action. The English prepositions "by, with, by means of" are generally used when translating this construction. Joan of Arc was executed "by means of" fire (i.e. burned at the stake). It may also be noted that *ignis, ignis* is a 3rd declension i-stem, the subject of chapter 20 of LFC, B. (See also AG, 409)

<u>necāvit,</u> perfect tense, 3rd person, sing. = it killed < necō, āre

    <u>damnāvit, necāvit</u> (it condemned, it killed) – Both of these verbs may be recognized by students of LFC. The forms seen here

are from the 3rd principal part, which is used to form the perfect tense (see chapter 2 of LFC, B). The perfect tense in Latin is best equated with the simple past in English.

Gallicus, a, um, adj. French   (cf. Gallia, France)

inquīsītiō, inquīsītiōnis, f., inquisition, investigation, inquiry

incipiō, incipere, to begin

quaesitor, quesitoris, m., inquisitor

Joan of Arc's Inquisitor, post mortem, was Jean Bréhal. The second investigation was begun shortly after the French drove the British from Rouen.

testis, testis, m/f., witness

documentum, ī, n., documents

perscrūtō, āre, āvī, ātum, to examine thoroughly, scrutinize

innocens, innocentis, adj., innocent

Adjectives of the third declension retain endings almost identical to those of 3rd declension i-stem nouns. Like all other adjectives, they too must agree with the noun modified in case, number, and gender. (See also AG, 114-119)

martyr, martyris, m./f., martyr

innocentem et martyrem, Predicate Accusative. This accusative phrase simply renames the direct object *Ioannam*. Thus it must agree with the noun modified by appearing in the accusative case also. (he declares Joan innocent and [a] martyr) (See also AG, 392 & 393)

dēclārō, āre, āvī, ātum, to declare

nam, adv., for

fraudulentus, a, um, adj., fraudulent

illicitus, a, um, adj., unlawful

iūdicium erat fraudulentum et illicitum. – The original trial was conducted by carefully selected pro-English clergy who were coerced into a guilty verdict. Jean Bréhal further determined the trial to have held illegal procedures and used intimidation of both the accused and the clergy presiding in order to obtain the verdict desired.

NOTA BENE:

septimō diē Iuliī – This date appears in accordance with our modern calendar. The Roman calendar would have dated this event in history as nonibus Iuliīs (the Nones of July). See the note regarding the Roman calendar in chapter 17, Magna Carta.

Respondē Latīnē:

1. Cūr prīmum iūdicium Ioannam damnat?

2. Quōmodo iūdicium adulēscentem necat?

3. Cūr secundum iūdicium Ioannam innocentem dēclārat?

cūr - why?
quōmodo - how?

CAPUT XXI

Annō MCCCLXXVIII, Pontifex Gregorius XI perit.

Turba cīvium Ītalōrum cardinalēs legere Ītalum

Pontificem suādent. Nam Ītalī cīvēs Pontificem manēre

in Sanctā Urbe avēbant. Sīc cardinalēs Urbanum VI,

cīvem Ītalum, legunt. Statim, Urbanus VI corrigere

ecclēsiam temptat. Is luxuriōsam vītam cardinalum

terminat. Īrātī cardinalēs Urbanum nōn amant. Eum

repudiant. Ēlectiōnem eius falsum propter turbam

cīvium, quam timēbant, dēclārant. Eōdem annō

cardinālēs novum Pontificum, Clementem VII, legunt.

Clemens et cardinālēs ad Galliam redeunt. Diū sunt

duō Pontificēs, deinde trēs. Dēnique, annō MCDXVII,

Concilium Constantiae ecclēsiam sub ūnō Pontifice

conciliābit.

Schisma Pontificum

GLOSSARY:

<u>pereō, perīre, periī, peritum,</u> to pass away, die < *per* + *eō, īre*

<u>cardinal, cardinalis,</u> m., cardinal

<u>legō, legere,</u> to pick out, choose

<u>Sancta Urbe</u> = Holy City, Rome

<u>corrigō, corrigere,</u> to straighten out, correct, reform

<u>temptō, āre, āvī, ātum,</u> to try, attempt

<u>luxuriōsus, a, um,</u> adj., extravagant, luxurious

<u>vīta, ae,</u> f., life or lifestyle

<u>repudiō, āre, āvī, ātum,</u> to scorn; reject

<u>ēlectiō, ēlectiōnis,</u> f., choice

<u>quam,</u> f, acc, sing. relative pronoun referring to *turbam* = whom

Relative pronouns take the gender and number of their antecedent (*turbam*), but their case is determined according to their use in the subordinate clause. *Quam* is the direct object of *timēbant* and is therefore placed in the accusative case.

<u>eōdem,</u> (eō + dem) demonstrative pronoun = that same

Students may recognize the ablative singular of the personal pronoun *is, ea, id.* This personal pronoun forms the base of the demonstrative pronoun *īdem, eadem, idem,* meaning "that same."

<u>Constantia, ae,</u> f., Constance

Schisma Pontificum

Respondē Latīnē:

1. Quī cardinalēs suādent?

2. Cūr cardinalēs Urbanum nōn amant?

3. Quis ecclēsiam conciliābit?

quī – who (plural)?
cūr – why?
quis – who?

CAPUT XXII

Iohannes Wicleffus & Iohannes dē Hussinetz
c. MCCCLXXX A.D.

In bibliothēca Pragae sunt tria numismata

sollemnia. In prīmō, Iohannes Wicleffus scintillās saxō

creat. In secundō, Iohannes dē Hussinetz flammam

scintillīs creat. In tertiō, Martinus Lutherus facem alte

tenet. Haec numismata sollemnia fābulam dē origine

Correctiōnis nārrant.

Iohannes Wicleffus Catholicam Ecclēsiam dē

multīs falsīs doctrinīs accūsat. Pontifex eum de haerese

accusat et eum propter hunc damnat et necat. Iohannes

dē Hussinetz etiam contrā falsās doctrinās ecclēsiae

adnūntiat. Hās accūsātiōnēs in librō, nomine <u>Dē

Ecclēsia</u>, dēmōnstrat. Tamen multī populī verba eōrum

crēdunt. Olim vir, nomine Martinus Lutherus, etiam

haec crēdit.

Iohannes Wicleffus & Iohannes dē Hussinetz

GLOSSARY:

<u>Iohannes dī Hussinetz</u>, nom., m., sing., John Huss (literally John from Hussinetz)

    Many men, such as John Wycliffe and John Huss, derived their surnames from the places in which they were born. The Latin name many times reflects this custom as with *Iohannes de Hussinetz* – John from Hussinetz.

<u>bibliothēca, ae</u>, f., library

<u>Praga, ae</u>, f., Prague

<u>numismata sollemnia</u>, nom., n., pl., medallions (literally – ceremonial coins)

    This triad of medallions on display in Prague date back to the year 1572.

<u>orīgō, originis</u>, f., origin

<u>Correctiō, Correctiōnis</u>, f., Reformation

<u>scintilla, ae</u>, f., sparks

<u>saxō . . . scintillīs</u> – These words are in the ablative case and are referred to as ablative of means or instrument. They are best translated using the preposition "with."

<u>fax, facis</u>, f., torch

<u>alte</u>, adv., high

<u>accūsātiō, accūsātiōnis</u>, f., accusation

<u>hunc, haec</u> – In the sentence 3rd from the end, *hunc* is being used as a demonstrative pronoun referring back to *librum*. In the final sentence, *haec* is also being used as a demonstrative pronoun to refer back to the *verba eōrum* in the previous sentence. This usage differs from the rest of the demonstratives in the passage, which are being used as adjectives modifying nouns.

<u>tamen</u>, adv., nevertheless

<u>nomine</u> = by the name of, called

Iohannes Wicleffus & Iohannes dē Hussinetz

Respondē Latīnē:

1. Ubī sunt tria numismata sollemnia?

2. Cūr Pontifex eōs damnat?

3. Quis verba eōrum crēdit?

ubī – where?
cūr – why?
quis – who?

CAPUT XXIII

Occāsus Byzantiī
MCDLIII A.D.

Byzantium est oppidum postrēmum Imperiī

Rōmānōrum. Muhammed II et Turcī Byzantium

oppugnant. Sunt multī Turcī et multa tēla nova habent.

Constantius XI, imperātor Byzantiōrum, paucōs virōs

habet. Tandem Byzantium, illum oppidum postrēmum

Imperiī Romanōrum, cadit.

Occāsus Byzantiī

GLOSSARY:

Byzantius, ī, m., Byzantine

Byzantium, iī, n., the city known as Constantinople, modern Istanbul

Turcī, Turcōrum, m.pl., Turks

tēlum, tēlī, n., weapon

Constantius XI, m., Constantine ("the ninth")

cadō, cadere, to fall

Respondē Latīnē:

1. Quī Byzantium oppugnant?

2. Quae habent Turcī?

3. Quis est Imperātor Byzantiōrum?

quī – who (plural)?
quae – what things?
quis – who?

CAPUT XXIV

Iohannes Gutenberg Biblia Imprimit
MCDLVI A.D.

Cum Iohannes Gutenberg erat iuvenis, specula

metallica creābat. Cum erat senior, machinam ad

imprimendum creābat. Illa māchina imprimere multōs

librōs poterat. Prīmus liber impressus erat enchiridion

Latīnae grammaticae. Secundus liber impressus erat

Latīna Biblia. Illa Biblia erant maior quam ista Biblia.

Singula Biblia in duōbus librīs imprimēbant. Necesse

erat ūtī prope trecentīs formīs. Erant XLII versūs

in quāque pāginā. Sīc, populī librum "XLII Versūs

Biblia" appellābant. Hodiē, illum "Gutenberg Biblia"

appellāmus.

GLOSSARY:

<u>cum</u>, the conjunction meaning "when" or "although"; not the preposition *cum* meaning "with."

<u>imprimō, imprimere</u>, to print

<u>speculum, ī</u>, n., mirror

<u>metallicus, a, um</u>, adj., metal

    The distinguishing factor in Gutenberg's press was the movable metal type, which did not wear out as fast as wooden type. It is thought that his earlier experience with metal work encouraged him in developing this feature.

<u>senior</u>, nom., m., sing., older

    This is a comparative adjective derived from the Latin word *senex*, old man.

<u>māchinam ad imprimendum</u> = printing machine (literally: machine for printing)

    The accusative of the gerund is used with the preposition *ad* to express purpose. (See also AG, 506)

i.e. *māchinam ad imprimendum creābat* = he began to create a machine for the purpose of printing.

<u>poterat</u>, imperfect of irregular posse = it was able

<u>impressus</u>, perfect passive participle = printed

    The fourth principal part of the verb *imprimere*, also known as the supine or passive participle. The participle in Latin, as in English, is a verb which operates as an adjective (see chapter 2, LFC B).

  i.e.: Q. What kind of book? A. The printed book.

<u>enchiridion, enchiridionis</u>, n., textbook

<u>grammatica, ae</u>, f., grammar

<u>maior quam</u> = bigger than

Here the comparative adjective *maior* is used with the conjunction *quam* in order to denote a comparison between two objects. (See also AG, 407)

illa Biblia . . . ista Biblia - Take note the use of the new demonstrative *iste* in contrast to the previously learned demonstrative *ille*.

singulī, singulae, singula, distributive adj. (always plural), single
These numerals are declined as the plural of 1st & 2nd declension adjectives (i.e. *bonus*). These are used instead of cardinals to modify a noun plural in form but singular in meaning. Such is the case with *Biblia* which is neuter plural in form but translates as the singular Bible. (See also AG, 136, 137)

necesse erat ūtī = it was necessary to use
ūtor, ūtī, (+abl.) to use This deponent verb must take an object in the ablative case.

prope, adv., nearly

trecentī, ae, a, cardinal numeral, three hundred

fōrma, ae, f., type (literally forms/shapes of letters)

versūs, (4th declension noun) nom. or acc., plural, masculine, line (of writing)
Each page of the Gutenberg Bible contains 42 lines of print. Thus, it was first known as the 42 Line Bible.

quāque, abl., f., sing., adj., each

Respondē Latīnē:

1. Ante machinās creat, quid Iohannes creābat ?

2. Quot versūs erant in ūnā pāginā?

quid – what?
quot – how many?

CAPUT XXV

Nova Auctōritās
c. MCCC - MLXVII A.D.

Diū ecclēsia erat auctor artium. Tum, circa

annum MCCC, multī populī omnia antīquae Rōmae et

Helladis conservābant. Ōratiōnēs Ciceronis, sapientiam

Platonis, et aedificia Vitruviī, architectī Rōmānī,

commemorant. Ante ars et doctrinae circum religiōnem

intendēbant, nunc hae circum hominem intendunt.

Haec nova auctōritās per Ītaliam et Europam ducentōs

annōs movet. Multī clārī artificēs per hōs annōs

habitant. Ūnus ex illīs virīs est Michaelangelō. Is

multās clārās statuās et picturās creat.

GLOSSARY:

omnia, acc., n., pl. = all things

      omnia, 3rd declension *omnis, omnis.* Third declension adjectives have endings almost identical to those of 3rd declension nouns. Here *omnia* acts as a substantive adjective. Substantive (*stō, stāre*) adjectives stand on their own without a noun. In the neuter plural the word "things" is usually implied.

      i.e. *omnia* = all things

Hellas, Helladis, f., Greece

Ciceronis, Platonis, Vitruviī, gen., m., sing., Cicero, Plato, Vitruvius

      Vitruvius was a renowned Roman architect and author of ***De Architectura*** (15 -13 B.C.). His surviving buildings were studied by Renaissance artisans. ***De Architectura***, all ten volumes, were printed and published in 1486. One volume was dedicated to theatre buildings and scenic displays.

architectus, ī, m., architect

ante, The students have learned *ante* as a preposition governed by the accusative case. Here, however, it is used as an adverb without an object.

doctrinae, ārum, f., (plural in form, singular in translation) science

      This word has many meanings: instruction, learning, education, science.

intendō, intendere, to focus

nunc, adv., now

ducentōs annōs, accusative of duration = for two hundred years

      This construction with the accusative is used to indicate a time period during which an event occurs.

statua, ae, f., statue

pictura, ae, f., picture

espondē Latīnē:

1. Quis est Vitruvius?

2. Circum quid nova auctōritās intendit?

3. Quae Michaelangelo creat?

uis – who?
uid – what?
uae – what things?

CAPUT XXVI

Inquīsītiō Hispāniae
MCDLXXVIII A.D.

Circā annum MCDLXXVIII, Inquīsītiō Hispāniae

sub regnō Rēgis Ferdinandī V incipit. Haec Inquīsītiō

Iudaeōs et Maurōs propter haeresēs eōrum damnat.

Auctoritātēs multa milia Iudaeōrum necant et pecūniās

eōrum sumunt. Pater Rēgis Ferdinandī mutuās

pecūniās ab Iudaeīs sumpserat. Iam fīlius illius eōs cum

sanguine repōnit.

Inquīsītiō Hispāniae

Prīmum, Pontifex Rōmānus, Sixtus VI, illam

inhūmānam Inquīsītiōnem Hispāniae nōn amat.

Ferdinandus, etiam Rēx Siciliae, Sanctam Rōmam

contrā hostēs nōn adiuvābit. Sīc, dubius Pontifex

benedictionem suam Inquīsītiōnī dare dēbet. Haec

horrenda Inquīsītiō in Hispānia trecentōs annōs

dūrābit.

Inquīsītiō Hispāniae

GLOSSARY:

Iudaeus, ī, m., Jew

Maurus, ī, m., Moor, Muslim, adherent of Islam

milia = thousands < pl. of mille

> **milia Iudaeōrum,** partitive genitive or genitive of the whole. This construction using the genitive case is used to express a part of something or of a group. The partitive genitive may not be used with any number except for *mille, milia* (thousand, thousands). See chapter 17 of LFC, B.

sūmō, sūmere, to take up

mutuās pecuniās sumpserat ab + ablative = he had borrowed money from . . .

> Literally translated: "he had taken borrowed money from the Jews." The phrase *sūmere mutuās pecuniās ab* may be simply translated as, "to borrow money from . . ."
>
> King Ferdinand's father, John II of Aragon, borrowed a great deal of money from wealthy Jews in order to finance arrangements for his son's marriage to Queen Isabella of Castille.

repōnō, repōnere, to put back, replace; (money) repay

prīmum, adv., first, at first

inhūmānus, a, um, adj., inhuman

Sicilia, ae, f., Sicily

> **Rēx Siciliae** – Ferdinand V was not only King of Spain alongside Queen Isabella, but he was also King of Sicily, neighbor to Italy. This gave him a point of great advantage in his persuasions with the Roman Pope. The Pope needed the King of Sicily as an ally against foreign invaders.

benedictio, benedictionis, f., blessing

suus, a, um, adj., his own

dēbeō, dēbēre, (+ infinitive) ought, must (best translated here as "must")

trecentōs annōs, accusative of duration of time = for three hundred years

dūrō, āre, āvī, ātum, to endure, continue

Inquīsītiō Hispāniae

Respondē Latīnē:

1. Sub regnō cuius erat Inquīsītiō Hispāniae?

2. Quōs Inquīsītiō damnat?

3. Cūr Pontifex benedictionem dat?

cuius – whose?
quōs – whom?
cūr – why?

CAPUT XXVII

Martinus Lutherus
MDXVII A.D.

Martinus Lutherus erat monachus Augustinī

in Catholica Ecclēsia. Theologiam in ūniversitāte

Germāniae docēbat. Ibi, epistulam Rōmānīs perscrūtat.

Legit, "iūstitia enim Deī in eō revelātur ex fide in fidem

sicut scriptum est; iūstus autem ex fide vīvit (Rom.

I.XVII)." Nunc Lutherus in Deō, quī iūstitiam propter

fidem nōn labōrēs dat, crēdit. Lutherus XCV thesēs

scrībit. Eōs in ianuā castellī pōnit. Multī hominēs

eōs vident et crēdunt. Catholica Ecclēsia Martinum

Lutherum excommunicat. Nunc, is est sacerdōs in

Ecclēsiā Urbis, primā Correctā Ecclēsiā.

Martinus Lutherus

GLOSSARY:

Martinus Lutherus, m., Martin Luther

This Latinization of Luther's name is taken from the *Assertiōnem Septem Sacramentōrum* (Assertion of the Seven Sacraments) written by King Henry VIII and Thomas Moore. You will read more about these three men and this document in Chapter 29, **Dēcrētum Imperiī.**

theologia, ae, f., theology

universitas, universitatis, f., university

Germānia, ae, f., Germany

iūstitia, ae, f., righteousness

enim, adv., for

revelātur, passive voice = it is unveiled < revēlō, āre, to unveil

fides, fideī, f., faith

scriptum est, perfect passive = it has been written < scrībō, scrībere, to write

vīvo, vīvere, vixī, victum, to live

quī, nom., m., sing., relative pronoun, who

thesis, thesis, f., thesis (plural = theses)

ianua, ae, f., door

castellum, ī, n., castle

excommunicō, āre, āvī, ātum, to excommunicate

sacerdōs, sacerdōtis, m/f., priest

Ecclēsia Urbis = City Church (literally-church of the city)

The City Church, located in Wittenberg, Germany, was the first reformed church in the world. Luther served as a priest and preached here for many years.

Martinus Lutherus

correctus, a, um, adj., reformed

      This word is taken from the fourth principal part of the verb *corrigō, corrigere,* also known as the supine or passive participle. The participle in Latin, as in English, is a verb which operates as an adjective (see chapter 2, LFC Primer B). *Correcta* is used here as an adjective modifying *ecclēsia.*

Respondē Latīnē:

1. Quam epistulam Lutherus perscrūtinat?

2. Quot thesēs Lutherus scrībit?

3. Ubī eās pōnit?

quam - which?
quot - how many?
ubī - where?

CAPUT XXVIII

Zwingli et Anabaptistatēs

MDXXV A.D.

Zwingli, pastor ecclēsiae Turicī, multōs iuvenēs

dē Graecā linguā et litterīs docēbat. Hī discipulī

Graecum Novum Testamentum perscrūtābant. Quīdam

baptismam līberōrum et missam repudiant. Pastōrem

suum repudiāre illās suādent, sed is illās nōn repudiābit.

Creāre ecclēsiam volunt, ubī Christianī Deum līberē

adorant, sīcut ecclēsiam Novī Testamentī. Zwingli,

Zwingli et Anabaptistatēs

autem, cum eīs discrepat. Multī eōs "Anabaptistātēs"

appellant, quod adultōs hominēs iterum baptizant.

Auctoritatēs ecclēsiae Anabaptistatēs propter haec

damnant, et eōs in flūmine summergunt.

Zwingli et Anabaptistatēs

GLOSSARY:

<u>Anabaptista, Anabaptistatis</u>, m., Anabaptist < from the Greek, ἀναβαπτίζω

    The word "Anabaptist" is derived from the Greek words ἀνα (again) + βαπτίζω (I immerse). The Anabaptists did not believe that the baptism of a child was sufficient. The recipient of the baptism must instead be a willing participant able to freely choose Christ and His church. Thus many members of the Anabaptist movement were re-baptized as adults.

<u>pastor, pastōris</u>, m., shepherd; pastor (leader of a congregation)

<u>Turicus, ī</u>, m., Zurich

<u>baptisma, ae</u>, f., baptism, submersion

<u>missa, ae</u>, f., mass (ecclesiastical)

<u>ubī</u>, adv., where

<u>līberē</u>, adv., freely

<u>adorō, āre, āvī, ātum</u>, to worship

<u>volunt</u> = they wish < volō, velle, irregular verb, to wish, want

<u>discrepō, āre, āvī, ātum</u>, to disagree

<u>adultus, a, um</u>, adj., grown, adult

<u>baptizō, āre, āvī, ātum</u>, to baptize

<u>flūmen, flūminis</u>, n., river

<u>summergō, summergere, summersī, summersum</u>, to submerge, drown

    Submergere is a compound verb constructed from the preposition *sub* (under) + the verb *mergere* (to dip, sink, plunge). Opponents of the Anabaptists seemed to find drowning a fitting style of execution for this particular form of heresy.

Zwingli et Anabaptistatēs

Respondē Latīnē:

1. Quis est Zwingli?

2. Quid Zwingli docet?

3. Quid iuvenēs repudiant?

quis – who?
quid – what?

Dēcrētum Imperiī

MDXXXIV A.D.

Thoma Morus est litteratus vir et Cancellarius

Britanniae. Thoma doctrinās Martinī Lutherī oppōnit.

Rēx Henricus VIII, amīcus Thomae, etiam illās doctrinās

oppōnit. Simul "Assertiōnem Septem Sacramentōrum

adversus Martinum Lutherum," dēfensiōnem

Catholicae fideī, scrībunt. Pontifex Rōmānus rēgem

laudat et eum "Dēfensōrem Fideī" appellat.

Dēcrētum Imperiī

Olim, autem, Rēx Henricus VIII novīs nuptiīs

cum Annā desiderat, quod sua uxor, rēgīna, fīlium

sibi nōn dabit. Pontifex Rōmānus repudiat. Īrātus

Rēx dicit, "Pontifex nōn est caput ecclēsiae Brittaniae,

ego sum! Quisquis negāre mē audēbit, illī in perīculō

erunt!" Rēx Thomam et aliōs obsignāre Dēcrētum

Imperiī iubet. Thoma dēcrētum nōn obsignābit. Sīc

Rēx Henricus Thomam Morum necat.

Dēcrētum Imperiī

GLOSSARY:

<u>Dēcrētum Imperiī</u> = Act of Supremacy

<u>Thoma Morus</u>, m., Thomas Moore

    This Latinization of Moore's name is taken from the *Assertiōnem Septem Sacramentōrum* (Assertion of the Seven Sacraments). *Thoma* like *agricola* is a masculine noun of the 1ˢᵗ declension.

<u>Cancellarius, ī</u>, m., Chancellor

    This Latin word, from which Chancellor is derived, literally means "doorkeeper." The Lord High Chancellor, the office occupied by Sir Thomas Moore, presided over the chancery, one of the five divisions of the High Court of Justice of Great Britain.

<u>oppōnō, oppōnere, opposuī, oppositum</u>, **to oppose** < *ob* (in front of) + *pōnere* (to put, place). To place yourself in front of someone is to oppose them.

<u>simul</u>, adv., together

<u>dēfensio, dēfensiōnis</u>, f., defense

<u>assertiō, assertiōnis</u>, f., assertion

<u>sacramentum, ī</u>, n., sacrament

<u>adversus</u>, preposition + acc., contrary to, against

<u>Assertiōnem Septem Sacramentōrum</u> - This document, originally written in Latin, was penned almost entirely by Sir Thomas Moore, although King Henry VIII's name appeared as author. The purpose of the document was to refute the attacks made by Martin Luther on the sacraments of the church. The document defended, among other things, the sacrament of marriage and the supremacy of the Pope. For this great written defense, the Pope bestowed upon King Henry VIII the title, "Defender of the Faith."

<u>dēfensor, dēfensōris</u>, m., defender

<u>novīs nuptiīs desiderat</u>, idiomatic expression = he desires a new wedding

    In this Latin idiom, *novīs nuptiīs* acts as the object for *desiderat*.

Dēcrētum Imperiī

<u>sibi</u> = to him < sui

    This is a reflexive pronoun, a pronoun that refers back to the subject of the sentence. Reflexive pronouns must be used in place of the personal pronoun, *is, ea, id* when referring back to the subject. (cf. *suus, a, um, his own*)

<u>ego</u>, nom., sing., pronoun = I

    The placement of the personal pronoun alongside the first person *sum* was used by the Romans to give special emphasis to the subject.

<u>quisquis</u>, nominative pronoun, whoever, everyone who

<u>dēcrētum</u>, ī, n., decree, act

<u>**Rēx Henricus Thomam Morum necat**</u> - Moore's refusal to sign the Act of Supremacy was counted as treason. He was imprisoned in the Tower of London and later beheaded by order of the king.

Respondē Latīnē:

1. Quis est Cancellarius Brittaniae?

2. Quis est Rēx Britanniae?

3. Cūr rēx est īrātus?

4. Cūr rēx amīcum necat?

quis - who
cūr – why

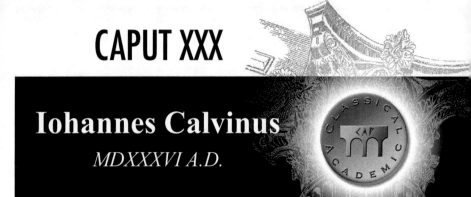

CAPUT XXX

Iohannes Calvinus
MDXXXVI A.D.

Iohannes Calvinus, annō dominī MDXXXII,

prīmum librum, <u>Dē Clēmentiā</u>, scrībit. Hic liber

opus, nomine etiam <u>Dē Clēmentiā</u> (scriptum ab

Senecā, philosophō Rōmānō), perscrūtat. In eō

Seneca consilium Imperātōrī Nērōnī dē clēmentiā

regnī eius dat. Brevī tempore, Calvinus relinquere

Catholicam Ecclēsiam et esse partem Correctiōnis optat.

Iohannes Calvinus

Deinde vicesimō tertiō diē Augustī, annō MDXXV,

Calvinus epistulam ad Rēgem Galliae scrībit. Epistula

clēmentiam prō Correctiōne rogat. Haec epistula erit

prōlogus magnī operis eius, <u>Institūtiō Christianae</u>

<u>Religiōnis</u>. Rēx clēmentiam nōn dabit. Sīc Calvinus

Genavam iter facit. Ibi manēbit et Ecclēsiam Correctam

fundābit.

Iohannes Calvinus

GLOSSARY:

<u>annō</u>, ablative of time = in the year . . .

<u>nomine</u> = called, by the name of

<u>clēmentia, ae</u>, f., mildness, compassion, mercy

<u>scriptum</u>, perfect passive participle = written

> This word is taken from the fourth principal part of the verb *scrībō, scrībere*, also known as the supine or perfect passive participle. The participle, in Latin as in English, is a verb that operates as an adjective (see chapter 2 in LFC, B). *Scriptum* is used here as an adjective modifying *opus*.

<u>Seneca, ae</u>, m., Seneca

> Seneca was a famous Roman philosopher and writer who served as Nero's beloved tutor in his youth, and later as an advisor during the early years of his reign.

<u>philosophus, ī</u>, m., philosopher

<u>Nērō, Nērōnis</u>, m., Nero

<u>brevī tempore</u>, idiomatic expression = in a short time, soon

<u>relinquō, relinquere, relīquī, relictum</u>, to leave, forsake

<u>vicesimō tertiō diē</u>, ablative of time when = on the twenty third day

<u>prōlogus, ī</u>, m., prologue

<u>Institūtiō Christianae Religiōnis</u> = Institutes of the Christian Religion

<u>iter facit</u>, latin idiom = he makes a journey, he travels

<u>Genavam</u>, accusative of place to which = to Geneva < Genava, ae, f.

<u>Ecclēsiam Correctam</u> = Reformed Church

> The supine or 4th principal part of *corrigere* is here used as an adjective to describe *ecclēsiam*. Calvin is credited with establishing the Reformed Church of Geneva which served as a base for the Reformation movement and the birth of Calvinism.

NOTA BENE:

<u>vicesimō tertiō diē Augustī</u> – This date appears in accordance with our modern calendar. The Roman calendar would have dated this event in history as ***a.d. X Kalendas Septembrēs*** (ten days before the Kalends of September). See the note regarding the Roman calendar in chapter 17, **Magna Carta**.

Respondē Latīnē:

1. Quis est Seneca?

2. Quid est magnum opus Calvinī?

3. Cūr Calvinus Genavam it?

quid – what?
quis – who?
cūr – why?

CAPUT XXXI

Concilium Tridentum
MDXLV – MDLXIII A.D.

Cum Concilium Tridentī incipit, tertiō decimō

Decembris annō MDXLV, id duōs fīnēs in animō habet.

Prīmum, concilium haeresibus Correctiōnis respondēre

dēbet. Secundum, multa scelera ē Catholicā Ecclēsiā

āmovēre dēbet.

Concilium septem sacramenta et imperium

Pontificis Rōmānī affirmat. Id tōtās novās doctrinās

Correctiōnis (id est "sōlā scriptūrā," "sōlā fidē," et cētera)

repudiat. Dēcrēta Conciliī Tridentī tōtās doctrinās et

trāditiōnēs Catholicae Ecclēsiae, sed nullās Correctiōnis

affirmant. Dēnique, Concilium Correctiōnem

"anathema" dēclārat. Multī ducēs Europae partem modo

dēcrētōrum cōgunt. Gallia tōta dēcrēta repudiat.

Concilium Tridentum

GLOSSARY:

<u>Tridentum, ī, n.</u>, Trent

<u>tertiō decimō diē</u>, ablative of time when = on the thirteenth day

<u>December, Decembris, m.</u>, December

<u>in animō habet</u>, idiomatic expression = it has in mind (it plans)

> This phrase is a Latin idiom often used in reference to the plans men make.

<u>respondeō, respondēre, respondī, responsum</u>, (+ dat.) to reply to, answer

<u>sōlā scriptūrā, sōlā fidē</u> = by scripture alone, by faith alone

> These expressions refer to essential doctrines of the Reformation and are the basis for the movement's separation from and rejection by the Catholic Church.
>
> *"sōlā scriptūrā"* – A teaching of the Reformation that states that doctrines should be formed "by scripture alone," as opposed to the traditions of the Church and the pronouncements of the Pope.
>
> *"sōlā fidē"* – A teaching of the Reformation that states that salvation is "by faith alone" and apart from the good works of man and that man can never earn God's justification and salvation through good works.

<u>id est, et cētera</u> – Both of these phrases have been adopted into our modern culture as literary terms, and should be very familiar to students in their abbreviated forms.

id est (i.e.) = that is   et cētera (etc.) = and the rest, and so on

<u>trāditiō, trāditiōnis, f.</u>, tradition

<u>anathema</u> = accursed

> This ecclesiastical term, which means "doomed offering, accursed thing," came late into the Latin language. It is derived from the Greek verb, ἀνατίθημι – to put on (as a burden). The root word of this Greek verb is the equivalent of the Latin verb *pōnō*.

<u>cōgō, cōgere, cōēgī, cōactum</u>, to force, enforce

Concilium Tridentum

NOTA BENE:

tertiō decimō diē Decembris – This date appears in accordance with our modern calendar. The Roman calendar would have dated this event in history as *Idibus Decembribus* (the Ides of December). See the note regarding the Roman calendar in chapter 17, **Magna Carta**.

Respondē Latīnē:

1. Quid est prīmus fīnis Conciliī?

2. Quot doctrinās Correctiōnis Concilium affirmat? Nōminā ūnum.

3. Quot doctrinās Catholicae Ecclēsiae affirmat? Nōminā ūnum.

quid – what?
quot – how many?
nōminā – name (imperative of nōmināre – to name)

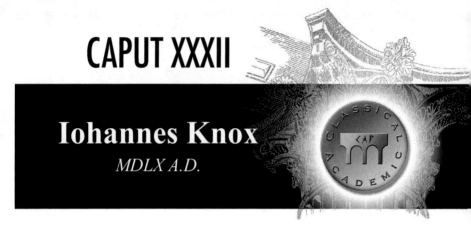

CAPUT XXXII

Iohannes Knox
MDLX A.D.

Iohannes Knox, nātus circā MDV, in Scotiā

habitābat. Gallicī oppidum eius oppugnant et eum

capiunt. Iam est servus et in nāve labōrat. Nautae sunt

saevī. Saepe eum verberant, deinde eum orāre Mariae,

mātrī Christī, cogunt.

Post duōs annōs, est līber. Prīmum ad Brittaniam

iter facit, deinde Genavam. Ibi cum Calvinō studet.

Iohannes Knox

Ducēs Correctiōnis in Scotiam eum redīre ad patriam rogant. Iohannes per Scotiam adnūntiat. Rēgīna Scotiae, Maria, est Catholica. Rēgīna Maria Iohannem nōn amat, sed illum timet; nam multī Scotī Iohannem amant et eius verba dē Christō crēdunt.

Iohannes Knox

GLOSSARY:

Scotia, ae, f., Scotland

capiō, capere, cēpī, captum, to seize, capture

verberō, āre, āvī, ātum, to whip, beat

iter facit, idiomatic expression = he makes a journey, he travels

Genavam, accusative of place to which = to Geneva < Genava, ae, f.

studeō, studēre, studuī, to study

Scotus, ī, m., Scotsman

Respondē Latīnē:

1. Quandō iter facit?

2. Ubī Iohannes adnūntiat?

3. Quis eum timet? Cūr?

ubī – where?
quandō – where, to what place?
quis – who?
cūr – why?

Appendix

Pater Noster
(The Lord's Prayer)

This prayer is taken from Matthew 6, vs. 9 – 13 of the Latin Vulgate. The word in [ ] has been added for clarity. This word does not appear here in the Vulgate, nor is it recited as part of the prayer.

Pater noster, quī es in caelīs, sanctificetur nomen tuum. Adveniat

regnum tuum. Fiat voluntas tua, sicut in caelō et in terrā. Panem

nostrum quotīdiānum da nobīs hodiē, et dīmitte nobīs dēbita

nostra sicut et nōs [dēbita] dīmittimus dēbitoribus nostrīs. Et ne

nōs indūcās in tentātiōnem, sed līberā nōs ā malō. Amen.

Appendix

GLOSSARY & NOTES:

*<u>sanctificetur</u> = let it be holy
*<u>adveniat</u> = let it come
*<u>fiat</u> = let it be so
<u>sicut et</u> = just as
<u>quotīdiānum</u>, adj., daily   (alternative spelling, *cottīdiānus*)
      While this adjective is used for the *Pater Noster*, it is interesting to note that the Vulgate uses the ecclesiastical adjective *supersubstantialem (life sustaining)* instead. However, *quotīdiānum* is a more accurate translation for the word ἐπιούσιον **(for the day)**, which is found in the original Greek tcxt.
<u>nobīs</u>, dative, indirect object = to us
      ablative of separation = from us
<u>dēbitoribus nobīs</u>, ablative of separation = from our debtors
      Note that the nouns *dēbita* and *dēbitor* are both related to the verb *dēbēre (to owe)*. A *dēbitum* is a thing "owed." A *dēbitor* is the person "owing."
*<u>ne . . . indūcās</u> = do not lead us
<u>tentātiōnem</u> < tentātio, tentātiōnis, adj., attack; trial, temptation

*Each of these verbs has been placed in the subjunctive mood. The jussive subjunctive is a more advanced construction that will be learned in years to come. The term "jussive" comes from the verb *iubeō, iubēre, iussī, (to order)* and is used to express a polite command or exhortation.

Venī, venī Emmanuel!
(O Come, O Come, Emmanuel!)

This ancient hymn is a unification of the great "O Antiphons."
These antiphons, devotional compositions sung responsively as
part of a church service, date back to at least the ninth century.
The antiphons were sung to the same melody in the second mode
of Gregorian chant. The five verses shown here are the original
five included in the hymn. Centuries later, two more were added
to form a total of seven. These are still sung or recited today
before and after the Magnificat at Vespers during the octave before
Christmas. You will notice that the imperative mood is used
quite frequently throughout. You may refer back to the lesson on
imperatives in chapter 28 of LFC, B if needed.

Venī, venī Emmanuel,

Captīvum solve Israel,

Quī gemit in exiliō

Prīvātus Deī Fīliō.

Gaudē, gaudē! Emmanuel

nascetur prō tē, Israel.

Venī, ō Jesse Virgula;

Ex hostis tuōs ungulā,

Dē specū tuōs tartarī

Dēdūc et antrō barathrī.

Gaudē, gaudē! Emmanuel

nascetur prō tē, Israel.

Venī, venī, ō Oriens

Solāre nōs adveniens;

Noctis dēpele nebulās

Dīrasque noctis tenebrās.

Gaudē, gaudē! Emmanuel

nascetur prō tē, Israel.

Venī clavis Davidica;

Regnā reclūde caelica;

Fac iter tūtum superum,

Et claude viās inferum.

Gaudē, gaudē! Emmanuel

nascetur prō tē, Israel.

Venī, venī Adonai,

Quī populō in Sinai

Lēgem dedistī vertice,

In majestate glōriae.

Gaudē, gaudē! Emmanuel

nascetur prō tē, Israel.

Appendix

GLOSSARY & NOTES:

venī, singular imperative < veniō, venire, to come

quī, nom., m., sing., who

nascetur = he is born

tuōs = your (people)

specū, abl., sing. < specus, ūs, m/f/n., cave, hollow

Oriens, vocative = Dayspring

    The vocative case is used for direct address, and often appears the same as the nominative case.

solāre = you save

    This is an alternative spelling for the second person singular of the deponent verb *solarī*.

adveniens, present participle = coming, arriving (modifies Oriens)

    Participles often act as adjectives and are used to modify nouns.

dēpele, imperative = disperse (alternative spelling: dēpelle)

caelica, adj., heavenly

tūtum, adj., watched over; safe, secure

superum, inferum, These adjectives are representative of Heaven (the place above) and Hell (the place below). The preposition *ad* should be understood with both of these accusatives.

dedistī, perfect tense of *dare* = you have given, you gave

vertice = from above

Glossary

"Numbers in parentheses indicate the chapter in which the word first appears."

ā, ab (15)	prep. + abl., from, away from
accūsātiō, accūsātiōnis (22)	f. accusation
accūsō, -āre, -āvī, -ātum (22)	1. accuse
ad (7)	prep. + acc. to, towar, near, by
adiuvō, -āre, -āvī, -ātum (26)	1, to aid, help
adnūntiō, -āre, -āvī, -ātum (16)	1, to proclaim, preach
adoptō, -āre, -āvī, -ātum (11)	1, to adopt
adorō, -āre, -āvī, -ātum (28)	1, to worship
adulēscēns, adulēscentis (16)	m/f. youth
adultus, -a, -um (28)	adj. adult, mature
adversus (29)	prep. + acc. contrary to, against
aedificium, -ī (6)	n. building
aedificō, -āre, -āvī, -ātum (6)	1, to build
Aegyptius, -a, -um (5)	adj. Egyptian
Aelfredus, -ī (9)	m. Alfred
aequē ac (28)	conj. just as, like
aevum, -ī (2)	n. age, time
affirmō, -āre, -āvī, -ātum (4)	1, to affirm
Africa, -ae (1)	f. Africa
ager, agrī (12)	m. field
Al-Coranus, -ī (7)	m. the Koran
alius, alia, aliud (2)	another, other

Glossary

alte (22)	adv., high
altus, -a, -um (22)	adj. high
amīcus, -ī (29)	m. friend
amō, -āre, -āvī, -ātum (21)	1, to love, like
āmoveō, āmovēre, āmōvī, āmōtum (31)	2, to move away, remove
anabaptista, anabaptistatis (28)	m/f. anabaptist
angelus, -ī (7)	m. messenger, angel
Anglī, -ōrum (13)	m.pl. the English (people)
Angulsaxon, Angulsaxonis (9)	m. Anglo-Saxon
animus, -ī (31)	m. mind, spirit
Anna, -ae (29)	f. Anna
annus, -ī (1)	m. year
ante (25)	adv. before, previously; prep. + acc. Before
antīquus, -a, -um (5)	adj. ancient, old
appāreō, appārēre, appāruī, appārītum (14)	2, to become visible, appear
appellō, -āre, -āvī, -ātum (3)	1, to call, name
Aquilōnarius, -a, -um (14)	adj. Northerly, Northern
Arabicus, -a, -um (7)	adj. Arabian
architectus, -ī (25)	m. architect
ars, artis (14)	f. art, skill
artifex, artificis (14)	m. artist
Asia, -ae (7)	f. Near East
assertiō, assertiōnis (29)	f. defence; declaration of civil status
Attila Hunnus (2)	m. Atilla the Hun
auctor, auctōris (7)	f. authority
auctōritās, auctōritātis (8)	f. authority, power
audeō, audēre, ausus sum	2, to dare
augeō, augēre, auxī, autum (5)	2, to increase
Augustinus, -ī (1)	m. Augustine

Glossary

Augustus, - ī (30)	m. August
aula, -ae (19)	f. court
aut (12)	conj. or; aut . . . aut = either . . . or
autem (11)	adv. however
auxilium, -ī (10)	n. help, aid
aveō, avēre (13)	2 (+ infinitive), to want eagerly
baptisma, -ae (28)	f. baptism
baptizō, -āre, -āvī, -ātum (28)	1, to baptize
barbarus, -ī (2)	m. barbarian, foreigner
baro, baronis (17)	m. baron
bellicōsus, -a, -um (2)	adj. warlike
benedictio, benedictionis (26)	f. blessing
Benedictus, -ī (5)	m. Benedict
beneficium, -ī (5)	n. benefit, gift
Bethlema, -ae (3)	f. Bethlehem
biblia, -ōrum (3)	n.pl. Bible
bibliothēcca, -ae (22)	f. library
bonus, -a, -um (8)	adj. good
brevis, breve (30)	adj. short, brief
Brittania, -ae (2)	f. Britain (Great Britain, including Wales & Scotland)
Byzantium, -ī (6)	n. Constantinople (modern day Istanbul)
Byzantius, -ī (6)	m. Byzantine
cadō, cadere, cecidī, cāsum (23)	3, to fall
cancellarius, -ī (29)	m. Chancellor
capillus, -ī (2)	m. hair
capiō, capere, cēpī, captum (32)	3, to seize, capture
caput, captitis (29)	n. head
cardinal, cardinalis (21)	m. cardinal
Carolus, -ī (8)	m. Charles
cārus, -a, -um (14)	adj. dear, expensive

Glossary

casa, -ae (12)	f. house
castellum, -ī (27)	n. castle
cathedralis (14)	adj. Cathedral
catholicus, -a, -um (11)	adj. catholic
causa, -ae (11)	f. cause, reason
caverna, -ae (3)	f. cave, cavern
centum (25)	adj. hundred
cēterus, -a, -um (31)	adj. the rest
Chalcedon, Chalcedonis (4)	f., Chalcedon
Christiānitas, Christiānitatis (16)	f. Christianity
Christiānus, -a, -um (5)	adj. Christian
Christiānus, -ī (5)	m. Christian
Christus, -ī (4)	m. Christ
cibus, -ī (5)	m. food
Cicerō, Cicerōnis (25)	m. Cicero, Roman orator and statesman
circā (5)	prep. with abl. around
circum (25)	adv. about, all around; prep. w/ abl. Around, about
cīvis, cīvis (21)	m/f - citizen
cīvitās, cīvitātis (8)	f. state, civlization, civilized society
clāmō, -āre, -āvī, -ātum (15)	1, to shout
clārus, -a, -um (3)	adj. bright, clear, famous
Clēmens, Clēmentis (21)	m. Clement
clēmentia, -ae (30)	f. mercy
cōdex, cōdicis (6)	f. book, notebook
cōgō, cōgere, coēgī, cōactum (17)	3, to force, enforce
commemorō, -āre, -āvī, -ātum (6)	1, to remember, commemorate
conciliō, -āre, -āvī, -ātum (10)	1, to bring together, unite
concilium, -ī (4)	n. council, gathering, meeting
confessiō, confessiōnis (1)	f. confession, acknowledgement
congregātiō, congregātōnis (16)	f. congregation, group

Glossary

congregō, -āre, -āvī, -ātum (4)	1, to gather
conservō, -āre, -āvī, -ātum (5)	1, to preserve, save
consilium, -ī (30)	n. plan; advice, counsel
Constantia, -ae (21)	f. Constance
Constantinopolis, Constantinopolis (2)	f., Constantinople
Constantius, -ī (23)	m. Constantine
contrā (22)	prep.w/acc. against
contrōversia, -ae (11)	f. controversy
convertō, converere, convertī, conversum (3)	3, to turn round; convert; translate
corōna, -ae (8)	f. crown
corpus, corporis (6)	n. body
correctiō, correctiōnis (22)	f. reformation
correctus, -a, -um (27)	adj. (ppp. of corrigere) reformed
corrigō, corrigere, correxī, correctum (21)	3, to straighten out, correct, reform
crēdō, crēdere, crēdidī, crēditum (7)	3, to believe
creō, -āre, -āvī, -ātum (4)	1, to create
cum (7)	prep. + abl. with; adv. when
cūr (4)	interrogative adv., why?
cūrō, -āre, -āvī, -ātum (12)	1, to care for, take care of
damnō, -āre, -āvī, -ātum (20)	1, to judge, condemn
Danicus, -a, -um (9)	adj. Danish
dē (1)	prep. + abl. down from, concerning, about
dēbeō, dēbēre, dēbuī, dēbitum (7)	2, to owe, ought, must
December, Decembris (30)	m. December
dēclārō, -āre, -āvī, -ātum (20)	1, to declare, announce
dēcrētum, -ī (29)	n. act, decree
dēfensiō, dēfensiōnis (29)	f. defense
dēfensor, dēfensōris (29)	m. defender

Glossary

dēfīnītiō, dēfīnītiōnis (4)	f. definition
deinde (2)	adv. then
dēmonstrō, -āre, -āvī, -ātum (22)	1, to point out, show
dēnique (2)	adv. then
dēsīderō, -āre, -āvī, -ātum (29)	1, to desire, long for
deus, -ī (4)	m. god
dīcō, dīcere, dixī, dictum (29)	3, to speak, tell
diēs, diēī (17)	m/f. day
difficilis, difficile (14)	adj. difficult
dīmittō, dīmittere, dīmīsī, dīmissum (16)	3, to send away, send forth
discipulus, -ī (16)	m. student
discō, discere, didicī (18)	3, learn
discrepō, discrepāre, discrepuī (28)	1, to disagree, sound different
diū (2)	adv. for a long time
dīvīnus, -a, -um (5)	adj. divine
dīvitiae, dīvitiārum (12)	f.pl. wealth, riches
dō, dare, dedī, datum (5)	1, to give
doceō, docēre, docuī, doctum (18)	2, to teach
doctrīna, -ae (4)	f. teaching, instruction, doctrine; science
documentum, -ī (20)	n. document
Dominicanus, -a, -um (18)	adj. Dominican
dominus, -ī (18)	m. lord, master
dubius, -a, -um (26)	adj. doubtful
ducentī, -ae, -a (25)	numerical adj. two hundred
duo, duae, duo (4)	numerical adj. two
dūrō, -āre, -āvī, -ātum (26)	1, to endure, continue
dux, ducis (10)	m. leader
ē, ex (5)	prep. + abl. out of, from
ecclēsia, -ae (6)	f. church
ēlectiō, ēlectiōnis (21)	f. election

Glossary

enchiridion, enchiridionis (24)	n. textbook
enim (27)	adv. truly
eō, īre, īvī / iī, ītum (7)	irreg. to go
episcopus, -ī (1)	m. bishop
epistula, -ae (27)	f. letter
ergō (8)	adv. therefore
et (2)	conj. and
etiam (1)	adv. even, also
Europa, -ae (2)	f. Europe
excidium, -ī (9)	n. destruction
excommunicō, -āre, -āvī, -ātum (27)	1, to excommunicate
exemplum, -ī (6)	n. example
exerceō, exercēre, exercuī, exercītum (5)	3, to train, practice
exercitus, -ūs (9)	m. army, infantry
expungō, -āre, -āvī, -ātum (2)	1, to expunge, cancel, remove
fābula, -ae (1)	f. story
faciō, facere, fēcī, factum (30)	3, to do, make
falsus, -a, -um (4)	adj. false
familia, -ae (12)	f. family
fastī, fastōrum, (7)	m.pl. calendar
faveō, favēre, fāvī, fautum (19)	2, (+ dative) to favor
fax, facis (22)	f. torch
fēmina, -ae (5)	f. woman
fides, fidēī (9)	f. faith
fīlius, -ī (11)	m. son
fīnis, fīnis (2)	m. end, goal
firmus, -a, -um (10)	adj. steady, secure
flamma, -ae (22)	f. flame
flāvus, -a, -um (2)	adj. yellow
flūmen, flūminis (28)	n., river, stream

Glossary

fōrma, -ae (24)	f. form, shape; type
fortis, forte (10)	adj. strong
Franciscus Assisiensis (16)	m. Francis of Assisi
frāter, fratris (16)	m. brother
fraudlentus, -a, -um (20)	adj. fraudulent
fraudō, -āre, -āvī, -ātum (14)	1, to deceive, cheat; (+ abl. of thing taken)
fuga, -ae (7)	f. flight, escape
fugiō, fugere, fūgī, fugitum (7)	3, to escape, run away, flee
fundō, -āre, -āvī, -ātum (9)	1, to found, establish
Gabriel, Gabrielis, (7)	m. Gabriel
Gallia, -ae (2)	f. Gaul (modern day France)
Gallicus, -a, -um (20)	adj. French
Genava, -ae (30)	f. Geneva, Switzerland
gens, gentis (2)	f. tribe, nation, race
genus, generis (14)	n. origin; class, kind; fashion, manner
germāna, -ae (12)	f. sister (full-blooded)
Germanī, -ōrum (2)	m.pl. Germans
Germania, -ae (27)	f. Germany
Germānus, -a, -um (2)	adj. German
germānus, -ī (12)	m. brother (full-blooded brother)
glōria, -ae (6)	f. glory
Gothicus, -a, -um (14)	adj. Gothic
Graecus, -a, -um (8)	adj. Greek
grammatica, -ae (24)	f. textbook
Gregorius, -ī (21)	m. Gregory
Guillemus, -ī (13)	m. William
habeō, habēre, habuī, habitum (2)	2, to have, hold
habitō, -āre, -āvī, -ātum (1)	1, to live, dwell
haeresis, haeresis (20)	f. sect, school of thought; heresy
Haroldus, -ī (13)	m. Harold

Glossary

Hastinga, -ae (13)	f. Hastings
Hellas, Helladis (25)	f. Greece
Henricus, -ī (29)	m. Henry
hic, haec, hoc (2)	pronoun/adj. this
Hierosolyma, -ōrum (15)	m.pl. Jerusalem
Hippo, Hipponis (1)	m. Hippo (town in North Africa)
Hispānia, -ae (2)	f. Hispania (modern day Spain)
historia, -ae (1)	f. history
hodiē (6)	adv. today
homō, hominis (25)	m. man
honorius, -ī (16)	m. honor
horrendus, -a, -um (26)	adj. horrendous
hostis, hostis (26)	m. enemy
hūmānitās, hūmānitātis (4)	f. human nature
hūmānus, -a, -um (4)	adj. humanity
iam (13)	adv. now, already
iānua, -ae (27)	f. door
ibi (5)	adv. there
ignis, ignis (20)	m. fire
ille, illa, illud (12)	pron./adj. that, those
illicitus, -a, -um (20)	adj. unlawful
imitātiō, imitātiōnis (16)	f. imitation
imperātor, imperātōris (6)	m. leader, general
imperium, -ī (2)	n. power, empire
impōnō, impōnere, impōsuī, impōsitum (17)	3, to place upon, impose
imprimō, imprimere, impressī, impressum (24)	3, to impress, print
in (1)	prep + abl. - in, on; prep + acc. - into
incipiō, incepere, incēpī, inceptum (20)	3, to begin
incipium, -ī (7)	n. beginning

ineō, inīre, iniī, initum (25)	irreg. to enter
infans, infantis (28)	m. infant
inhūmānus, -a, -um (26)	adj. inhuman
innocens, innocentis (20)	adj. innocent
inquīsītiō, inquīsītiōnis (20)	f. inquery investigation; inquisition
insidiae, -ārum (7)	f. pl. - ambush, trap, plot
intendō, intendere, intendī, intentum (25)	3, to focus
inter (9)	prep. + acc. - between, among
interdum (12)	adv. sometimes
interrogō, -āre, -āvī, -ātum (20)	1, to question
intrā (11)	prep. + acc. inside, within
Ioanna Darco (20)	f. Joan of Arc
Iohannes, Iohannis (10)	m. John
īrātus, -a, -um (11)	adj. angry
is, ea, id (5)	pronoun, he,she,it
Islamicus, -a, -um (7)	adj. Islamic
ita (24))	adv. thus
Ītalī, -ōrum (10)	m.pl. Italians
Ītalia, -ae (19)	f. Italy
iter, itineris (15)	n. journey
iterum (6)	adv. again
iubeō, iubēre, iussī, iussum (16)	2, to order
Iūdaeus, -ī (26)	m. Jew
iūdicium, -ī (20)	n. court, trial
Iūlius, Iūliī (20)	m. July
Iūnius, -ī (17)	m. June
iūstitia, iūstitiae (27)	f. justice
iūstus, -a, -um (17)	adj. just
iuvenis, iuvenis (24)	m/f. youth
Jerominus, -ī (3)	m. Jerome

Glossary

Justinianus, -ī (6)	m. Justinian
labor, labōris (27)	f. work
labōrō, -āre, -āvī, -ātum (6)	1, to work
Latīnē (6)	adv. in Latin
Latīnum, -ī (3)	n. Latin (the language)
Latīnus, -a, -um (3)	adj. Latin
laudō, -āre, -āvī, -ātum (29)	1, to praise
legō, legere, lēgī, lectum (12)	3, to pick out, choose; to read
lex, lēgis (6)	f. law
liber, librī (1)	m. book
līberī, -ōrum (12)	m.pl. children
līber, lībera, līberum (32)	adj. free
lingua, -ae (3)	f. tongue, language
littera, -ae (5)	f. letter of the alphabet; (pl.) literature, document
litterātus, -a, -um (3)	adj. learned
lītus, lītōris (2)	n. shore
lūdus, -ī (5)	m. game, school
luxuriōsus, -a, -um (21)	adj. luxurious
māchina, -ae (24)	f. machine
magister, magistrī (12)	m. teacher
magnus, -a, -um (2)	adj. great, large
Māia, -ae (20)	f. May
malus, -a, -um (16)	adj. bad
maneō, manēre, mansī, mansum (21)	2, to remain
Marcus Polo (19)	m. Marco Polo
Martinus Lutherus (22)	m. Martin Luther
martyr, martyris (20)	m./f. martyr
māter, mātris (1)	f. mother
Maurus, -ī (26)	m., Moor, Muslim, adherent of Islam
maximus, -a, -um (12)	superlative adj. great

Glossary

Medina, -ae (7)	f. Medina
medius, -a, um (2)	adj. middle
mercātor, mercātōris (19)	m. merchant
Merīdiānus, -a, -um (9)	adj. Southern, Southerly
metallicus, -a, -um (24)	adj. metallic, of metal
Michaelangelo, Michaelangelonis (25)	m. Michaelangeo, Renaissance artist
mīles, mīlitis (8)	m. soldier
mille, milia (26)	thousand, thousands
minor (16)	comparative adj. lesser, smaller
missa, -ae (28)	f. mass (ecclesiastical)
modo (13)	adv. only
monacha, -ae (5)	f. nun
monachus, -ī (3)	m. monk
monasterium, -ī (5)	n. monastery
Monica, -ae (1)	f. Monica
morbus, -ī (16)	m. sickness, illness
mors, mortis (10)	f. death
moveō, movēre, mōvī, mōtum (5)	2, to move
mox (5)	adv. soon
Muhammed, Muhammedis (7)	m. Mohammed
multus, -a, -um (1)	adj. many
mūtuus, -a, -um (26)	adj. borrowed, lent
nam (20)	adv. for
nārrō, -āre, -āvī, -ātum (1)	1, to tell
nātus, -a, -um (18)	adj. born
nauta, -ae (31)	m. sailor
nāvigō, -āre, -āvī, -ātum (2)	1, to sail
nāvis, nāvis (32)	f. ship
necesse (24)	indeclinable adj. necessary
necō, -āre, -āvī, -ātum (20)	1, to kill, execute

Glossary

negō, -āre, -āvī, -ātum (29)	1, to deny, reject
nōbilēs, nōbilium (5)	m.pl. nobility
nōmen, nōminis (22)	n. name
nōn (4)	adv. not
Normannī, -ōrum (13)	m.pl. Normans
Northmannī, -ōrum (2)	m.pl. Northmen, Vikings
nōs (8)	pronoun, we, us
nōtus, -a, -um (6)	adj. known
novus, -a, -um (5)	adj. new, strange
nullus, -a, -um (12)	adj. none, not any
nūmen, nūminis (4)	n. godhead, divine will
numisma, numismatis (22)	n. coin
nunc (25)	adv. now
nūntiō -āre, -āvī, -ātum (7)	1, to announce, proclaim, preach
nuptiae, -ārum (29)	f.pl. marriage, wedding
obscūrus, -a, -um (4)	adj. obscure, shady, unintelligible
obsignō, -āre, -āvī, -ātum (17)	1, to sign
occāsus, -ūs (5)	m. downfall, fall
Occidentalis, Occidentalis (9)	adj. Western
occupō, -āre, -āvī, -ātum (15)	1, to seize, attack
octō (15)	adj. eight
officium, -ī (5)	n. office, duty
ōlim (18)	adv. once upon a time, one day (in the future)
omnis, omne (25)	adj. all
opēs, opum (10)	f.pl. power, wealth
oppidum, -ī (1)	n. town
oppōnō, oppōnere, opposuī, oppositum (29)	3 to oppose
oppugnō, -āre, -āvī, -ātum (9)	1, to attack
optō, -āre, -āvī, -ātum (30)	1, to choose, wish
opus, operis (18)	n. work

Glossary

ōrātiō, ōrātiōnis (25)	f. speech, oration
orbis, orbis (2)	m. globe
ordo, ordinis (16)	m. order
Orientalis, Orientalis (11)	adj. Eastern
orīgō, originis (22)	f. beginning, origin
ōrō, -āre, -āvī, -ātum (1)	1, to pray, beg
Otto, Ottōnis (10)	m. Otto
paene (12)	adv. almost
paganus, -ī (9)	m. rural; pagan (as opposed to Christian)
pāgina, -ae (24)	f. page
pangō, pangere, panxī /pepegī, pepactum (9)	3, to fasten, settle
parātus, -a, -um (15)	adj. prepared, ready
pāreō, parere, paruī (7)	(+ dative) to obey
parō, -āre, -āvī, -ātum (5)	1, to prepare
pars, partis (8)	f. part
parvus, -a, -um (12)	adj. small, little
pastor, pastōris (28)	m. shepherd
pater, patris (11)	m. father
patria, -ae (32)	f. fatherland, native country
patruus, patruī (19)	m. paternal uncle
paucī, -ae, -a (7)	adj. (always plural) few
paupertās, paupertātis (16)	f. poverty
pax, pācis (9)	f. peace
pecūnia, -ae (14)	f. money
per (2)	prep. + acc. through
peregrinus, -a, -um (15)	adj. foreign
pereō, perīre, periī, peritum (21)	irreg. to perish, die
perīculum, -ī (29)	n. danger
perscrūtō, -āre, -āvī, -ātum (20)	1, to study thoroughly, examine
persōna, -ae (4)	f. person

Glossary

philosophus, -ī (30)	m. philosopher
pictūra, -ae (25)	f. picture
pirata, -ae (2)	m. pirate
Platō, Platōnis (25)	m. Plato, Greek philosopher
pōnō, pōnere, posuī, positum (27)	3, to put, place
pontifex, pontificis (8)	m. priest, pontiff (pope)
populus, -ī (3)	m. people, nation
possum, posse, potuī (24)	irreg. to be able, can
post (2)	adv. after, behind
posterī, posterōrum (5)	m.pl. posterity, future generations
posterus, -a, -um (15)	adj. the following, future
postrēmus -a, um (23)	adj. last, final
potestās, potestātis (17)	f. power
praeceptum, -ī (7)	n. rule; order, command
praedicō, -āre, -āvī, -ātum	3, to preach, proclaim
Praga, -ae (22)	f. Prague
prīmum (26)	adv. first, at first
prīmus, -a, -um (15)	adj. first
prīncips, prīncipis(13)	m/f. prince, leader
prō (1)	prep. + abl. for, on behalf of
probō, -āre, -āvī, -ātum (16)	1, to approve (of)
prōcēdō, prōcēdere, processī, processum (11)	3, to proceed
proelium, -ī (13)	n. battle
profānus, -a, -um (10)	adj. secular, not religious
prōlogus, -ī (30)	m. prologue
prope (3)	prep. + acc. near
propter (10)	prep. + acc. on account of, because of
proptereā (13)	adv. on account of this
puer, puerī (5)	m. boy
pulcher, pulchra, pulchrum (6)	adj. beautiful

Glossary

putō, -āre, -āvī, -ātum (11)	1, to think
quaerō, quaerere, quaesīvī, quaesītum (18)	2, to seek
quaesītor, quaesītoris (20)	m. inquisitor
quandō	interrogative adv., when?
quisque, quaeque,quodque (24)	adj. each
quī, quae, quod	interrogative adj. which, what?; relative pronoun - who, which
quīdam, quaedam, quiddam (14)	pronoun, a certain, certain ones
quinque (7)	adj. five
quis, cūius (1)	interrogative pronoun, who, which one?
quisque, cūiusque (24)	adj./pronoun, each
quisquis (29)	pronoun, whoever, everyone who
quō	interrogative adv., where, to what place?
quod (3)	conj. because
quot (15)	interrogative adj. (indeclinable) how many?
redeō, redīre, rediī, reditum (16)	irreg. to go back, return
rēgīna, -ae (29)	f. queen
regnum, -ī (19)	n. rule, reign; realm, kingdom
regō, regere, rexi, rectum (8)	3, to rule, govern
rē gula, -ae (5)	f. rule
religiō, religiōnis (7)	f. religion
relinquō, relinquere, relīquī, relictum (30)	3, to leave behined
repōnō, repōnere, reposuī, repositum (26)	to put back, repay
repudiō, -āre, -āvī, -ātum (21)	1, to scorn; reject, refuse
respondeō, respondēre, respondī, responsum (31)	2, to answer, reply to
revēlō, -āre, -āvī, -ātum (27)	1, to unveil, uncover; reveal

Glossary

rēx, rēgis (8)	m. king
Ricardus, -ī (17)	m. Richard
rīdeō, rīdēre, rīsī, rīsum (7)	2, to laugh, smile
rogō, -āre, -āvī, -ātum (10)	1, to ask
Rōma, -ae (2)	f. Rome
Rōmānī, -ōrum (2)	m.pl. Romans
Rōmānus, -a, -um (2)	adj. Roman
Rotomagus, -ī (20)	m. Rouen, France
sacer, sacra, sacrum (8)	adj. sacred, holy
sacredōs, sacerdōtis (27)	m/f. priest
sacrāmentum, -ī (29)	n. guarantee; sacrament
saeculum, -ī (2)	n. age, time
saepe (12)	adv. often
saevus, -a, -um (2)	adj. vicious, cruel
sanctus, -a, -um (5)	adj. holy
sanguis, sanguinis (26)	m. blood
sapientia, -ae (6)	f. wisdom
Saxo, Saxonis (2)	m. Saxon
saxum, -ī (22)	n. rock
scelus, sceleris (31)	n. evil deed, crime
schisma, -ae (11)	f. schism, division
schola, -ae (8)	f. school (an advanced school; not the grammar or elementary school called the *lūdus*)
scintilla, -ae (22)	f. spark
sciō, scīre, scīvī, scītum (3)	4, to know
Scotia, -ae (32)	f. Scotland
Scotus, -ī (32)	m., Scotsman
scrībō, scrībere, scripsī, scriptum (1)	3, to write
scriptūra, -ae (7)	f. writing, scripture
sectātor, sectātōris (7)	m. follower, adherent
secundum (30)	adv. second, next, following

Glossary

secundus, -a, -um (2)	adj. second
sed (13)	conj. but
sella, -ae (14)	f. chair
semper (16)	adv. always
Seneca, -ae (30)	m. Seneca, a Roman philosopher and instructor to Nero
senior (24)	comparative adj. - older
sēparō, -āre, -āvī, -ātum (11)	1, to separate, divide
septem (29)	numerical adj. seven
septimus, -a, -um (20)	adj. seventh
serva, -ae (10)	f. slave
sīc (10)	adv. thus
Sicilia, -ae (26)	f. Sicily
sīcut (16)	adv. just as
silva, -ae (16)	f. forest, wood
simul (29)	adv. together, at the same time
Sina, -ae (19)	m. Chinese
sine (16)	prep. + abl., without
singulī, -ae, -a (24)	distributive pl. adj. a single (set of something)
socius, -ī (2)	m. ally
sollemnis, sollemne (22)	adj. solemn, ceremonial
sōlus, -a, -um (11)	adj. only, alone
somnium, -ī (7)	n. dream, daydream, nightmare
somnus, -ī (5)	n. sleep
speculum, -ī (24)	n. mirror
spīritus, -ūs (11)	m. spirit
spoliō, -āre, -āvī, -ātum (2)	1, to plunder, rob
statim (21)	adv. immediately
statua, -ae (25)	f. statue
studeō, studēre, studuī (32)	2, to study
suādeō, suādēre, suāsī, suāsum (15)	2, to suggest; urge

Glossary

sub (10)	prep. + abl. under; prep. + acc. up under, beneath
subiungō, subiungere, subiunxī, subiunctum (10)	3, to harness, bring under the control of, subjugate
sum, esse, fuī, futūrum (1)	irreg. to be
summergō, summergere, summersī, summersum (28)	3, to submerge, drown
summus, -a, -um (18)	adj. highest, greatest
sūmō, sūmere, sumpsī, sumptum (26)	3, to take up
superō, -āre, -āvī, -ātum (2)	1, to overcome
suus, -a, -um (26)	adj. his own
symbolus, -ī (11)	m. symbol, mark, (in ch. 11) creed
tamen (22)	adv. nevertheless
telum, -ī (23)	n., weapon
temptō, -āre, -āvī, -ātum (21)	1, to try, test, temp
tempus, temporis (10)	n. time
teneō, tenēre, tenuī, tentum (22)	2, to hold
terminō, -āre, -āvī, -ātum (17)	1, to limit
terra, -ae (2)	f. earth, land
tertius, tertia, tertium (22)	adj. third
testāmentum, -ī (28)	n. will, testament
testis, testis (20)	m./f. witness
theologia, -ae (27)	f. theology
thesis, thesis (27)	f. thesis (pl. theses)
timeō, timēre, timuī (21)	2 to fear, be afraid of
Thoma, ae (18)	m. Thomas
tōto (15)	adv., in all, in total
tōtus, -a, -um (4)	adj. whole
trāditiō, trāditiōnis (31)	f. handing over; tradition
trecentī, -ae, -a (24)	numerical adj. three hundred
trēs, tria (21)	numerical adj. three

Glossary

rīcēsimus, -a, -um (20)	numerical adj. thirtieth
Tridentum, Tridentī (31)	n. Trent
urba, -ae (21)	f. mob, crowd, disturbance
Turcī, -ōrum (23)	m. Turks
Turicum, -ī (28)	n. Zurich (Switzerland)
bī (3)	interrogative adv., where; conj. - where, when
ūniversitās, ūniversitātis (27)	f. university
ūnus, -a, -um (1)	adj. one
Urbanus, -ī (15)	m. Urban
urbs, urbis (20)	f. city
uxor, uxōris (7)	f. wife
Vandalī, -ōrum (2)	m pl. Vandals
astō, -āre, -āvī, -ātum (2)	1, to lay waste to, destroy, desolate
astum, -ī (5)	n. desert, wasteland
ectīgal, vectīgālis (17)	m. tax
Venetianus, -a, -um (19)	adj. Venetian
erberō, -āre, -āvī, -ātum (32)	1, to whip, beat
erbum, -ī (7)	n. word
ersus, -ūs (24)	m. line, verse
īcēsimus, -a, -um (30)	numerical adj. twentieth
icis (10)	f. return, recompense
ictor, victōris (13)	m. conqueror
ictoria, -ae (15)	f. victory
ideō, vidēre, vīdī, vīsum (27)	2, to see, watch
īgintī (17)	numerical adj. twenty
ir, virī (2)	m. man
Vitruvius, -ī (25)	m. Vitruvius, Roman architect
isigothī, -ōrum (2)	m.pl. Visigoths (Western Goths)
īta, -ae (1)	f. life, lifestyle
īvō, vīvere, vīxī, victum (27)	3, to live

Glossary

vocō, -āre, -āvī, -ātum (8)	1, to call
volō, velle, voluī (12)	irreg. to wish, want
vulgātus, -a, -um (3)	adj. common

About the Authors

Karen Moore began her study of Latin in seventh grade, and added Greek to her linguistic studies during her college years. In 1994, she was awarded the Ruth and Myron G. Kuhlman Scholarship in Classics by the University. Karen graduated from the University of Texas at Austin in 1996 with a Bachelor of Arts in Classics and a minor in History. Since that time she has taught Latin to students in grades three through twelve through a wide variety of venues, including home school, public school, and Classical Christian schools. She is currently serving as the Latin Chair at Grace Academy of Georgetown, a Classical Christian School located in the heart of Texas. Karen and her husband, Bryan, have three children who attend school at Grace Academy.

Erin Davis graduated Magna Cum Laude in 2001 from Hillsdale College with a Bachelor of Arts in Classics. While at Hillsdale, Erin spent her junior year studying in Athens, Greece. In 2003, she earned a Master of Arts in Classics from the University of California at Santa Barbara. Since that time Erin has taught Latin, Greek, Classical Civilization, and Humanities courses at Classical Christian schools in central Texas. She and her husband, Jeremy, currently reside in Austin where Erin teaches at Hill Country Christian School of Austin.

About the Editor

William Nethercut is Professor of Greek and Latin and of Egyptology at the University of Texas in Austin, Tx. He holds degrees from Harvard, Columbia University, and the New England Conservatory of Music. He has taught at Columbia University, the University of Georgia, and, for the last 30 years, at the University of Texas.

ANSWER KEY

**Looking for the answers to this book?
Download and print the answers (PDF)
for <u>free</u> from our website at:**

www.ClassicalAcademicPress.com

Are you looking for an understandable, engaging, and creative way to introduce your students to the ancient language of the New Testament? *Greek for Children, Primer A* has been designed to teach the language with the lively structure and methods perfectly suited to grades three and up.

Koine Greek is a rich and fascinating language. It will aid students in critical thinking skills and a strong understanding of grammar. Many English words are derived from ancient Greek, and students will especially see the benefits of studying Greek when studying science and medicine. Last, Koine Greek is the language of the New Testament, and the study of the original language will gradually unveil the richness, depth and beauty of Scripture. *Greek for Children, Primer A* is comprised of thirty two chapters, to be completed one per week. Each chapter includes a worksheet and a quiz.

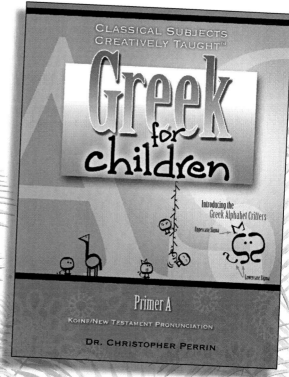